# PRESUMED GUILTY

The Tim Wilkes Story

# PRESUMED GUILTY

## The Tim Wilkes Story

by
Ben Greer

Wyrick & Company

*This book is dedicated to the memory of*
*Lila Castles Wilkes*

Published by Wyrick & Company
P. O. Box 89
Charleston, South Carolina 29402



Printed and bound in the United States of America

Library of Congress Cataloging-in-Publication Data

Greer, Ben.
Presumed guilty : the Tim Wilkes story / by Ben Greer.
p. cm.
Includes bibliographical references and index.
ISBN 0-941711-29-3 : $18.95
1. Wilkes, Tim—Trials, litigation, etc. 2. Trials (Bribery)--South Carolina. 3. Political corruption—South Carolina. I. Title.
KF224.W547G74 1994
364.1'323—dc20
[B]

94-36249
CIP

# Preface

In the summer of 1990, I read in *The State* newspaper about a federal sting called Operation Lost Trust. At the time, I was not exactly smitten with curiosity. However, in the next few months the revelations of the sting became scandalous, thereby arousing my interest.

By the spring of 1991, any number of black sins had been reported and I was eagerly awaiting further illuminations. Around this time, I became aware of a fellow named Tim Wilkes. He was described by *The State* as a roué, a hedonist, perhaps a sybarite—my kind of man. The more I read about him, the more I liked him. He was honest, witty, a boxer, a surfer, a painter, both urbane and provincial. Having always been beguiled by ambiguity, I decided to write his story, if he would allow me.

This book is intended to be a work of art as well as an historical account of Tim Wilkes' involvement in Operation Lost Trust. The people and dates and events are real, although a few names have been changed. Sometimes the dialogue has been re-created, either because I did not know what was actually said or because I wanted to achieve a more powerful sense of drama. For instance, I did not consult the courtroom transcripts of the trial, but relied upon Tim Wilkes' recollection of his and other testimony.

*Presumed Guilty*, then, is my impression of Tim Wilkes' recollections of a traumatic episode in his life. It is also a warning to all who might assume that our government is always our friend.

B.G.

# PRESUMED GUILTY

## The Tim Wilkes Story

# 1

In the beginning, it felt like any other summer morning in Winnsboro.

I awoke around five A.M. It's my usual time to get up. Ever since I was an eight-year-old kid sweeping out the Economy Drug Store before school, I felt like if I could get up earlier than everybody else, get a head start, I'd have the advantage for the rest of the day.

I was staying in my guest house. It's a small place behind my main house on Vanderhorst Street. It's kind of a playhouse really. I have a combination bedroom-sitting room. There's a small kitchen and beside it my workout room. Here I keep my heavy bag, my weights and bench press. At the far corner is a jacuzzi.

Having downed one or two glasses of wine the night before, I jumped out of bed and went straight for the heavy bag. I put on my worn leather mitts, wiped a little sleep from my eyes and started pounding the bag hard. I did a little dancing, some foot work, and threw a bunch of punches until I worked myself up slick.

I had started boxing a little in high school and continued in college. I was 42 now and most of my buddies had long ago given up the sport, but not me. I liked it. It kept me quick and hard and light. It gave me an edge.

After the workout was coffee. I love good coffee. A couple years earlier, I had bought a state-of-the-art Krups coffee maker. It could make cappuccino and tea and a couple other things I hadn't even heard of. The machine looked like something out of a physics lab: white enamel with stainless steel knobs and gauges and dials. I started the process, then headed for the jacuzzi.

It was blue-green and sat three steps above the floor. If you've never been jacuzzied in the morning, you ought to try it. It gets everything hot and loose and ready for action. I slipped down into the tub and started planning my day.

In a few minutes I could smell the coffee. I splashed a little bit more, dried off and put on my terry cloth robe. I poured me a cup of the best coffee in South Carolina and headed out the door to walk in my garden.

There were several different roses blooming: Mister Lincoln's, Angel Face and Golden Showers. I take great pride in my rose garden. I've got over 150 bushes, and I planted and nurtured each and every one. A rose, a rosebush is a work of art. You must tend it patiently and carefully and if you do your job well, then you create a thing of beauty which will reward you.

I bent down and smelled a fresh American Beauty, then strolled over and looked at the burgundy blooms on a crape myrtle. They grow throughout the backyard. It's important for me to do this, to take the early morning and pause and appreciate the things which come up from the earth. If you don't do this, I think you miss one of the secrets of life.

In a few more minutes, I went back into the house and put on a brand new Armani suit, Bally shoes and a silk tie. I was ready to take on the world.

My house sits one street behind Main. So in the mornings, I usually walk over to the Tavern. It's a restaurant which sits in a red brick building. The building used to house one of the oldest theatres in the state. Just as I crossed Main Street, an elderly man stopped me. He was wearing faded overalls and scuffed work boots.

"Representative Wilkes, how are you this morning?"

"Fine, Amos, how's your garden coming?"

"Good. Way too good, I got to bring you some tomatoes."

The old man put his hand on my shoulder. "You know, Mister Wilkes, I hate to bother you this morning, but you remember my grandbaby, Teddra? Well, she's applied to the University and she's got real good grades and all, but she sure could use a good word from you."

"Does she need a reference letter?"

"Yes, sir, I think so."

"Well, you find out exactly what she needs and bring the information by my office."

He shook my hand and smiled and before I could get ten feet further, another man stuck out his hand.

"Tim, that's a good looking suit. Who's your

tailor?"

"I buy 'em off the rack, Red."

"Hell, by the looks of it, I couldn't even afford that."

Red Thomas worked in the mill. I'd known him most of my life. He had just got laid off.

"Can I take a minute of your time?"

"Sure."

"Tim, I swear I got to get a job. Can you help me?"

"Yeah, listen, I hear they got some openings at the gold mine. I'll put in a good word for you. Make a couple of calls this afternoon."

Red Thomas talked on a bit and I listened and promised to try and help him find some work.

This is the way my life is and I thrive on it. Almost every place I go someone stops to speak to me. And it's not always to ask for something. A lot of times it's just to chat about sports or the crops or what's going on at the State House. I love people. I think you have to love them if you're going to be a good politician. You have to like to talk and laugh and commiserate and listen. If you're going to be successful, you have to listen more than anything else because through listening, you hear the heartbeat of your community. You need to know what's happening on the streets.

Once I sat down in the Tavern, Polly Parker came over and asked me what I wanted and I just said breakfast. Whatever she fixes is good. I rarely ask for anything specific. I got a paper and quickly went through it, making sure I hadn't said anything the day before that had gotten me in trouble. I believe in speaking my mind, particularly on important issues, but sometimes I say a little too much. Or speak a little too brashly. I don't apologize for this. It's the way I am and it gets things done, but occasionally the press picks up on a casual remark and I get kicked.

By the time I'd finished the paper, Polly brought the breakfast over. It was hash browns and fried eggs and sausage and biscuits. There was also a dish of pear preserves. They were beautiful to look at. They sat amber and granular and gleaming in a little glass bowl. Before I touched anything else, I put a spoonful of them on a hot biscuit and tried not to stick the whole thing in my mouth at once. Polly's pear preserves and biscuits are a little bit of heaven in Dixie.

While I was eating, Gordon, Jimmy Ray and "Snooks" sat down and we talked about everything from roses to racehorses. Before I knew it, an hour was gone and I paid and sprinted for the door, promising "Snooks" I'd show him how to get black spot off his rose bushes.

I was halfway to the office when Janus stopped me. He's a fella who makes me a little nervous. He wore blue jeans and a plaid shirt, but it was what dangled around his neck that gave me the creeps: it was a necklace made out of yellow bones and broken glass. The pendant was an upside down crucifix.

Janus is the classic small-town character, but there's something else about him, something about the way his green eyes look around you. I've heard it said he can tell the future.

Janus motioned me over to a bench in front of

the Courthouse. He was wearing a cowboy hat with a long black feather stuck in it. On the brim were written the numbers—666.

"Tim, I hate to tell you this, but I got some right bad news."

"What's that?"

His green eyes looked at me and he grinned. "The devil's looking for you, Tim."

"Now Janus..."

"Saw him this morning and I'm telling you he's looking for you."

Then Janus started speaking in tongues, his eyes rolled back in his head.

"Janus, you don't fool me, you're a lot smarter than you let on, everybody knows that. You must..."

"Well, I can't be too damn smart cause I'm sitting here beside you on this bench when I know the devil's looking for you."

With that, he jumped up and grabbed his hat and scurried away.

I shook my head and walked on, but I felt something. I don't know what it was really, but I felt that Janus knew something.

By the time I got to my office, I was wringing wet. Even though it was only 7:30 in the morning, the temperature was over 80 degrees and the humidity was stifling.

I said good morning to my secretary, Annette, and went straight into my office. It was a mess. I had just won my first reelection as the representative from my district. Posters and placards were scattered all over the place. There were red, white and blue handbills and fliers and stacks of large black and white pictures of me.

I was about to start tidying up when Annette knocked on my door.

"It's here," she said.

"What's here?"

"You know."

A delivery man hauled in a tall box.

It didn't take me long to open it.

There she was—six feet of blue-and-white speed. It was a new surfboard I had bought in Hawaii. For a few minutes, I looked at her and ran my hands along the smooth loveliness of her design.

Finally, I stood the board in the corner and started making some phone calls.

After about two hours, there was another tap at the door.

"Tim, there are two men here to see you."

"Who?"

"I've never seen them before."

"Ask them if they have appointments. I'm really behind here."

I was aggravated. I thought they were some sort of salesmen, but as soon as I saw them, I knew I was wrong. They wore blue suits and dark shoes and were a little too neat. They had an air about them, a kind of surliness. I stuck out my hand.

"Hey, how y'all doing?"

One of them smiled, shook my hand. "We need to talk to you."

"Well, I'm on my way to Columbia. I'm late. Who are you with?"

"We need to talk to you right now, Mister Wilkes."

"Look, I don't want to be impolite here, but..."

The one who wasn't talking reached inside his coat and flipped out a badge. Now, I've seen a lot of badges in my life, but not one like this: it was a big, thick blur of blue and gold.

"F.B.I., Mister Wilkes. Think we could have a little bit of your time?"

My mouth probably dropped open a little, and I said: "Well, I think I might find a little time for you fellas."

They came into the office and sat down. The one who was doing the talking pulled out a piece of paper and said, "We're conducting a little survey, Mister Wilkes."

"A survey?"

"Yeah."

"Well, what kind of survey?"

At this point, I wasn't scared, wasn't shaking in my boots or anything. I guess I was mostly just curious. They started asking about cash payments. Had I received any cash payments from lobbyists? I didn't like the sound of that because "cash payments" has a certain connotation about it. A cash payment implies that there will be some kind of an exchange for money, like: I'll give you X amount of dollars and you do this for me.

So they kept asking questions from a piece of paper, and then they got into cash campaign contributions and how they are reported.

I said, "Well, now, wait a minute. Are you

talking about cash payments or cash contributions? There's a big difference."

"We're talking about cash payments."

"Would you give me a copy of those questions you're asking?"

"Nope."

"Why not? I'd just like to see exactly what you're asking."

The agent leaned back in the chair and wiggled a finger in his ear, then inspected it.

"Can't do it."

I said, "Well, could you read me the questions and let me write them down?" So they let me do that.

I read over the questions and said I had not received any cash payments, but I had received cash contributions and so had every other politician in the United States, including the President.

They then asked from whom I had received contributions and I said several sources, and that my records were scattered all over—some in Columbia, some in Winnsboro and some in my car.

"Look, are you investigating me?" I asked.

"There's an investigation. That's all we can say."

"Do I need a lawyer?"

"Up to you, but we don't think so."

They then handed me a subpoena and told me I had until three P.M. that afternoon to gather my records for them to pick up.

After they had left, I still wasn't sure if I was the one being investigated. Maybe that sounds a little odd, but they had not made it clear whether they were after me or some lobbyist or even one of my clients.

Anyway, I called one of my business partners at my office in Columbia, Bill McDowell. I told him what had happened. What he said was very simple: "You need to get yourself a lawyer. You need to get yourself the best lawyer there is."

Driving down to Columbia, about a 30 minute trip, I was racking my brain. What was this about? Were they after me? If so, why? I had done nothing wrong. I was certain of that. And then I began to think—well, maybe, I had done something wrong. I'm brand new at this political game and maybe I've made some kind of dreadful mistake that I don't know about.

When I got to my Columbia office, I told my secretaries to get everything, every record boxed up. After a couple of hours, I called the F.B.I. and told them to come get them.

What I had no knowledge of then, but I later found out, was the following: at exactly 11 o'clock on July 18, 1990, 40 F.B.I. agents hit the offices of 18 state legislators, including me. The raid was planned with the accuracy of a military attack. Nothing was left to chance. There were no phone conversations among F.B.I. agents before the operation. All secretaries working for the F.B.I. were sworn to silence and forced to sign affidavits confirming this. There were no written memos. Everything was conducted in absolute secrecy.

When the trap was sprung, all I heard was the snap of the jaws. The pain of the wound and the knowledge of it would come later.

At this point in my life, my girlfriend, Katherine Courtwright, and I were not getting along. We weren't broken up exactly, but we had had a fight and she had gone with her mother to New York on a shopping trip. So here I was late in the afternoon in Columbia with the temperature near a hundred degrees, not a breath of air, the trees drooping in the heat, even the birds hidden from the relentless sun. Here I was—besieged by the F.B.I., confused by the sequence of events, and alone. Completely alone.

After a while, I called up Russell Munn, an old friend. I told him what had happened, and he said to come to his house for supper, that I didn't need to be alone.

I went over and we had a couple of drinks and I told him more about what had happened during the day. Russell at that time was a lobbyist for the State Chamber of Commerce and a high-profile guy, so he was very interested—very concerned, I should say.

At seven o'clock, we turned on the news on WIS TV. There, standing in front of the State House, was reporter Jerry Adams telling the story of a federal sting and naming the names of those implicated. A couple of minutes into the story, they flashed a hundred dollar bill up on the screen—I don't mean a small one either—a big, one hundred dollar bill. In the center of it, instead of Benjamin Franklin, was a picture of me.

I couldn't believe it. Neither could Russell or Harriet, his girlfriend. There was my picture in the center of that hundred dollar bill as if I were the ring leader, the number one guy. No one at WIS had called me. No one had interviewed me. No one had asked me anything. They had simply taken me and hung me on the screen. It was a lynching. There was no investigation, no evidence, no defense, no trial, just: hey, let's get Tim Wilkes and hang him. This was the first glimmer I had that the system—and by that I mean the electronic media and the print media and the legal system—was all wrong. Later, I would find out how wrong.

Towards the end of the news story, which went on and on about state legislators and corruption and cash payoffs, Jerry Adams said something to the effect that Representative Tim Wilkes had stated that he forgot about the money he was given by a well-known lobbyist. Well, that simply was not true. Adams had not even talked to me. WIS didn't know it, but I had already gotten an extension to file an amended legislative disclosure form because of cash contributions and expenses. I was careful with the money that people had given me. I was a first-term legislator and a certified public accountant. I was concerned about doing things exactly right, about not making one mistake. I felt like the people of my district had put their faith in me, had elected me and I wanted to be the best and the brightest legislator they had ever had.

Well, I was just in agony, sitting in front of that T.V., thinking: everybody in the whole state is watching this. Everybody in the whole state will think I'm guilty because of this. I was outraged, mad, embarrassed and for one of the few times in my life, I was afraid. At that very moment, I decided I was going to do something. Maybe it was a move I learned from boxing: when a guy hits you hard, you counterpunch just as hard. Anyway, I called up WIS and set them straight.

About ten minutes later—I think it was in the middle of the weather—the anchorman came on with a retraction. He said that earlier in the broadcast one of their reporters, Jerry Adams, had said some things about Representative Tim Wilkes which were incorrect. He said that I had, in fact, not given any statement and their reporter had not even interviewed me. He apologized for the statements of Jerry Adams.

That helped a little, I guess, but here I was sitting in the living room with my friends listening to the news, trying to figure out what in the world had happened, and this guy comes on and tries, convicts, and sentences me without ever having asked me a word about it.

Later, after everyone at Russell's house had gone to bed, I kept asking myself: why *me*? Why did the media focus on *me*? At some point the answers came. I've always been a person who stood up for things he believed in. I've always spoken my mind and I haven't been afraid to tangle with anybody, not even the Governor when I felt I was right. I have an attitude and have developed a certain notoriety that makes for good copy and now I was paying a dear price for it.

The night was awful. I don't mind saying that I got a little drunk. It's all I could do. I needed somebody. Maybe it's not a masculine thing to say, but I needed somebody to hold me and say it's gonna be all right, you're gonna be all right, but nobody was there. I had no family close by. I couldn't get in touch with my girlfriend. I was alone. I've never felt so alone.

I remember I got up at some point and went out and stood on the porch. It was a hot night, but I didn't feel the heat. I felt cold. I felt a horrible sense of coldness.

There was moonlight shining through the pine trees. I could hear a mockingbird singing. I have heard them singing in moonlight all my life, but that night the music sounded strange and mournful and cold. Almost like it was a dirge. Almost like it was saying: *say goodbye*. Goodbye to your career, to your friends, to the whole struggle of your life.

In the middle of July, surrounded by hot darkness, I remember how very cold it was.

I started thinking back, back to my early days, back to Brooklyn, New York.

# 2

It was a tough neighborhood. We lived down near the docks. I can remember the sound of tugboat horns, the shrieks of oil tankers and the bellows of passenger ships. It was a world of work and the air was rich in the smells of it: the stench of chemicals and soot and gasoline; the odor of fish and oysters; sweet bananas gleaming on the deck of a tramp steamer; oranges and pineapples and tangerines; and sometimes when the wind was right, the milky smell of the sea.

My mother's was one of those classic stories. Lila Castles was a talented, beautiful young woman and more than anything else in the world, she wanted to be a star, to be famous, to be somebody. She had 12 brothers and sisters and lived on a little dirt farm in Blackstock, South Carolina. As a child, she read movie magazines and went to movies when she could afford them. By 18, she was determined to be an actress. So, against everyone's advice, she got on the train and went to New York City in the summer of 1938, just 19 years old.

I don't know how far she got with her career. I know that she met Desi Arnaz and Joe DiMaggio and other celebrities. She frequented clubs like the

Copacabana and went to Rockefeller Center. According to my Aunt Louise, she tried out for a part in a Broadway play, but she didn't get it.

It was around this time—the time when Mama was losing some of the stars in her eyes—that she met my Dad.

There's not a lot to know about him. The person in the family who knows the most is my cousin, Bill Castles, a professor at the University of South Carolina. I've talked with him about Daddy and, of course, Mama had her own stories about him. Neither Mama nor cousin Bill knew when Daddy was born or who his parents were. All Mama ever said was that he was an orphan, a street kid raised in the rough and tumble of New York City. It was the time of the Great Depression. An Englishman, a Mister A. A. Wilkes, took a shine to the kid. Eventually, he adopted my father and suddenly there was this little guy named Alan Dale Wilkes.

Daddy seems to have been raised well. He was even sent to college somewhere in the City. He got a degree in journalism, and when Mama met him, he was a writer for the Associated Press. Mama had given up on her acting career and was attending Columbia University and trying to get a business degree. They started dating. It was about 1940, I think. Mama said that he was very handsome and charming and that he was a good writer and that she loved his creativity as much as anything else. Sometimes in the evenings they would go down to Mulberry Street in Little Italy and eat carbonara and spumoni and she would read Daddy's newspaper stories out loud to him, which he seemed to like.

Things were going pretty well between them until the war came. Daddy said that he had to go. Mama did everything she could to change his mind, but he was stubborn. They got married, and soon after, he left for Europe.

He fought in the European Theatre for two years and was wounded. He came home with a Bronze Star, a Silver Star and a Purple Heart. People said he was never the same after that. He began to drink.

My brother Robin was born first and then I came along in 1948. We lived down on the waterfront in Brooklyn. Cousin Bill Castles came to see us a number of times and later said that our living conditions were pretty bad. We lived in the basement of an old tenement right down on the water. Even though I was very young, I can still feel the cold wet of that place.

The wharf rats were what bothered me the most. I can still remember them. You would see them at night a lot. They were big, big as cats, and they had scabs and sores on their bald tails and a lot of them had big, orange eyes. They weren't scared of anything. You could clap your hands or even throw a rock and they didn't even move; they just looked at you with those orange eyes.

Mama said that rats were so bad that people had to make sure and wipe all the milk from their babies' mouths at night or the rats would creep down into the cribs and eat away the children's lips.

It was 1951, and Mama was still working on a business degree at Columbia University and Daddy was working two jobs: a reporter in the daytime and a detective—or at least that's what he said—at night. Around this time, he started to get abusive. He stayed out way too late at night. He was drinking. Mama told me that he beat her and wasn't a good father to me and Robin. Things were bad.

Years later, Bill Castles told me just how bad. Bill used to come up to New York in the summers. I think he was working on his Master's degree at the time. He would work and save money during the year and then he would come up to see Broadway plays in the summer. One year he stopped, without warning, at our apartment to say hello. Usually he called to let us know he was coming by, but this time I don't think he did.

Bill said that a stranger opened the door and the first thing that he saw was a pile of cash. The room was full of smoke and whiskey. Daddy was sitting at the table with two other men. He wasn't cordial to Bill at all. The men sitting around the table were rough. They wore nice suits and all, but, according to Bill, they looked bad and there were guns on the table.

Bill went back through the apartment looking for Mama. The place was a mess—leaky ceilings and plaster falling off the walls. He found Mama and Robin and me in a back room. He said my brother and I were skinny and pale and that Mama looked very bad. He visited a while, asked if he could help in any way, but Mama was proud and said, no, things were fine.

Bill Castles was a family man, a man interested in and concerned about his family. He was then and he is now. When he got back to South Carolina, he went straight to my Mama's family in Blackstock and he told them what he had found in that ugly tenement on the waterfront.

Mama's family was living in my Grandmother Castles' old, rambling farmhouse. A number of her children still lived with her. The first one Bill Castles talked to was my Uncle Spratt. He was a tough man. There were a lot of men like him in South Carolina in the late '40s. They were raw-boned, sinewy, dirt farmers who knew what hard living was all about. They were the kind of men you didn't mess with. Uncle Spratt, like my Grandfather, was a blacksmith. He knew how to make iron do anything he wanted it to. When Uncle Spratt heard Bill's story, the decision was made to go get us and bring us home. Uncle Spratt and two of my aunts got on the train at Chester and went to New York City.

Exactly what happened, I'm not sure of. There was talk that my Daddy wasn't a detective at all. There was talk that he was a gangster. There certainly wasn't a shootout or anything; I would have heard about that. Uncle Spratt brought his baby sister, Lila, and Robin and me back home. No one left a note for Daddy, but I guess he pretty much figured out where we were. Within two days, he appeared at the train station in Chester. Now this was a New Yorker, born and bred. He had never been to the South before. No one told me so, but I feel sure he was carrying a gun with him.

Word got out pretty quick that he was in town. When Uncle Spratt heard about it, he told his brother Fred. They threw their shotguns in the back of the pickup and headed for the train station. I sure would have liked to have seen that: the New York gangster slowly walking down Main Street towards the two country boys cradling double-barrel shotguns in their arms.

Somehow or other, no shots were fired. Uncle Spratt made it clear that his sister and her children were staying. Daddy apparently accepted the situation and returned to New York. We never heard from him again. A couple of years later he was found dead on the streets of the City. In the mail, Robin and I received our only inheritance: a Silver Star, a Purple Heart and a picture.

# 3

The morning after the State House sting story broke, I drove back to Winnsboro from Russell's house. I was confused and hurt, hung over and angry and not knowing what to do. I was totally without direction. I tried to call Kenny Goode, my best friend and lawyer, forgetting that he had gone out of town.

I came back to the safety of my house. I called Barbara Harmon. She had helped to raise me and was my second mother. I went to see her and she was just distraught. I got the paper and there I was in living color. I had tried to blot the shock out the night before with liquor, but here it was again. It was real and there was nothing I could do.

I tried everything. I got in my jacuzzi and made a pot of coffee, but the thing wouldn't go away. I was still wet and threw myself on the bed, not believing that this was happening.

I reached for the phone and called my office. I spoke to Annette. She said the place was bedlam. People were calling, coming by. Everybody in the office had a copy of the newspaper. No one was working. She said that every newspaper, radio and T.V. station in the state had called—even CNN. At least I had enough sense not to speak to them.

I got my clothes on and tied my shoes—both major accomplishments.

I worked in my rose garden and cleaned the swimming pool. I did everything I could to stay out of the house and stay away from the dreaded ring of the telephone.

Around two o'clock, I went over to the Tavern to get a sandwich. There were several people there. I felt incredibly awkward, and perhaps for the first time in my whole life I felt shy, like I didn't want to see anyone. I had to shake hands with a number of people. The ones who had seen the news stories looked at me apologetically. The others were as friendly as ever. It was strange. I could tell immediately who had seen the news and who had not. No one said a word. It was in their faces, in their eyes—the way they would half smile, drop their eyes and look away. I had never felt this from people in my life. It hurt me about as much as anything else. I didn't blame them for it. I was their Representative. I was the guy who was supposed to look after them and help them and fight their battles, and here I was accused of selling my vote. For a moment, I almost felt ashamed. Then I thought—for what? You haven't done anything. You are innocent. There is nothing for you to be ashamed of.

Late that same afternoon, Kenny Goode came to my house. He was my best friend. I grabbed and hugged him and told him what had happened. It turned out he had heard some of the story on the radio. I must have asked him a thousand questions, but at one point I stopped and looked at him hard.

"I'm innocent, Kenny. I didn't do what they're accusing me of."

"I know you are."

"So what do I do?"

"You get a lawyer."

"You're my lawyer."

"You need me and somebody else—somebody who understands the federal court system better than I do. Somebody who scares people. You need Gedney Howe."

While Ken scheduled an appointment with Gedney, I immersed myself in the unfolding story.

Clark Surratt wrote a story on July 19 in *The State* newspaper which stated that federal agents had issued subpoenas on Wednesday, July 18 for campaign and economic disclosure records for all 124 South Carolina House members in an investigation of cash contributions for legislative favors. A number of individual House members also received subpoenas for their campaign records—I was one.

The investigation involved possible violations of the Hobbs Act, a federal anti-corruption law that prohibits legislators' acceptance of money or gifts in return for promised performance. Apparently, there was a central figure in the sting—someone who was acting as a lobbyist; someone who was conducting the entire operation and offering money for legislative favors.

After digesting this bit of news, I sat back and wondered who this person could be. I knew a lot of lobbyists. Further reading suggested that legislators may have been videotaped or photographed in meetings with the mystery man.

The next day was terribly unsettling. I kept wondering who the secret lobbyist was. I also kept recalling *The State* newspaper's statement that certain legislators might have been videotaped. Was I on videotape? And if so, where had the taping taken place?

I spent the morning talking to Barbara Harmon and her mother, Mrs. Virginia McFadden. They were my next door neighbors. When I had been a little boy, these two women had fed me and educated me and bound up all the bruises of my life. My mother was a wonderful person, but had a drinking problem and sometimes I had needed all the care that Barbara and Mrs. Virginia could give. They were still giving it, and I felt like I needed them now more than ever.

Just before I was supposed to drive down to Charleston to meet with Gedney Howe, I heard on the news that the mysterious lobbyist had been identified. His name was Ron Cobb. I had met him several times. The knowledge of this scared me because during two of our meetings, he had given me $1500 in cash. It was a campaign contribution, but I knew I had to be on tape now. I had come to his office on the top of the AT&T building across from the State Capitol in Columbia.

I immediately called Ken Goode and told him that the lobbyist had been identified and that I knew him and had received money from him. Ken told me that I needed to make all of this very clear to Gedney.

I put down the phone and, full of apprehension, went to see Kenny. This was another trait that I developed. Anytime I heard anything new about the sting, I ran straight to Ken and asked him questions. As soon as I got to his office, I gave him the story reporter Levona Page had written about Ron L. Cobb.

I left Ken Goode's office and drove down to Charleston. Thinking about what I had read, I was at once horrified and fascinated. As I said, I had met Ron Cobb, but he wasn't a friend of mine. I knew that he was a libertine, that he lived a meretricious life. I wondered exactly what his role was in the sting and what he would say about me. Again the thought shuttled through my mind: did he have me on video tape? What did I say to him? What were my exact words?

I floored the accelerator. I wanted to get to Gedney Howe quick.

Gedney was born in Charleston. He was the son of a successful man who built a famous law firm. Gedney had gone to work in the firm once he got out of law school and he had made it even more successful. He bought one of the great houses of Charleston—the Calhoun Mansion—and restored it. He filled the house with ornate antiques. He wore conservative, handmade suits and elegant ties. He owned a Mercedes and a Rolls Royce and kept a summer house at McClellanville. He loved to eat French cuisine at the finest restaurants in Charleston. He was so socially prominent that when Prince Charles came to Charleston, he visited Gedney at the Calhoun Mansion. Judges and governors and senators all courted Gedney because of his intellect and his impeccable taste and his connections. He was one of—if not *the*—most powerful, most feared, most sought-after lawyers in the state of South Carolina.

Gedney's office sits in the historic district of Charleston on Chalmers Street. It is in an old restored fire station made of brick and stucco. Inside, the place is filled with ancient oil paintings and antiques. The rugs are deep and old and handmade. There are cloisonné vases and glittering chandeliers. It is one of the most beautiful offices I have ever seen. But when I walked into it, I thought, how very different we are. I like to wear Italian suits. I blow-dry my hair, wear contacts and keep a year-round suntan.

Gedney could not be more different in his appearance: dark suits, striped ties, white shirts, short hair and glasses, and a demeanor which suggests aristocracy and quiet pride and old world charm, though behind all of this gentility there is a feeling of laser intellect, a feeling which suggests to those who meet him—don't tread on me.

After Gedney had shown me about his impressive office, we went to a late lunch. It was exactly the kind of place I thought he would take me—a small, French bistro. There were linen tablecloths and finished oak floors and croissants on fine china. If he had come to meet me, we would have gone to a place with formica tables and linoleum floors and big, old yellow biscuits on an odd saucer.

We sat down and ordered some kind of fancy dish and then went straight to business.

"I think I need to tell you something right off," Gedney said.

His accent had a rich, Gullah inflection.

"I don't like fuckin' politicians. I've never liked them."

I looked at him a moment, then I smiled. "Well, I think I need to let you know something. I don't like fuckin' lawyers—and I don't know many people who do."

Gedney Howe is a man who is not used to being talked back to. I saw his intelligence rouse, collect and muster.

"Don't think I don't know all about you, Wilkes. You're a cocky, arrogant, showboating s.o.b., and that is a well-known fact."

"And you are a pompous, silver spoon, stuffed shirt with a fake accent, and that is a well-known fact."

"All politicians are the same."

"So are lawyers."

"You're just interested in politics and your own self- aggrandizement."

"Lawyers are interested in money—other people's money."

I think the waiter brought the salad then. We sat and glared at each other—the aristocrat and the redneck. Our faces were fierce and our teeth were bared and our minds were working. I was thinking: how in the world could Kenny set me up with this pluperfect snob. I don't care how many cases he's won and how well connected he is and how many princes have slept in his house, I ain't gonna work with him.

"By the way, this is going to cost you quite a lot," Gedney said.

"How much?"

"Fifty thousand."

"Fifty thousand dollars?"

"You're in a lot of trouble."

"Well, I don't have fifty thousand dollars."

"Better get it. And I want all of it up front, right away."

"Why?"

"Because you're in serious trouble and it will require serious thinking and that costs serious money."

"Look, I think you should give me a little discount here. This is going to be a big case. I think it will be the biggest case of your life. It'll make you money in the future."

Gedney put his linen napkin to his mouth and said, "Let's get one thing straight, Wilkes. I don't need you. You need me."

We got through lunch, then went back to Gedney's office, where he proceeded to tell me that he was certain the U.S. Attorney was going to proceed.

"What does that mean exactly?" I asked.

"He will indict and prosecute you and everyone else named as a target in the sting."

"He can't."

"What do you mean he can't?"

"I'm innocent."

"So what?"

"You cannot indict an innocent man."

"You better get over that notion right now. You are not seen as an innocent man by the U.S. Attorney. You are guilty and have to prove your innocence."

On the way back to Winnsboro, I was fuming. Whatever happened to the idea that you are innocent until proven guilty? I thought that was the way the law worked: every American is innocent before the law until he is proven guilty. They can't indict me. They won't indict me. This kind of thing does not happen in this country. There are laws. There's the constitution. If you are innocent, you are protected, and I am, so I will be fine. They can't lay a hand on me.

The questions steamed through my mind. What was this investigation going to do to my business? What would it do to my political career? How would it affect my friends, like Kenny Goode and Mrs. McFadden and Barbara Harmon? And what about my girlfriend? How about Katherine? Would she stay with me?

These questions continued all that day and into the night. At one point, I even became paranoid about my prospective lawyer Gedney Howe, a paranoia that would resurface many times. Maybe he wanted the fifty thousand up front because he knew the case would never go to trial and he wanted to get his money quickly—in my mind, the best case scenario. Or maybe he would let the case cook along slowly just to prove to me that he was working, when, in fact, it was clear to all that I was innocent and would never be indicted. Or worse, even worse, what if Gedney was in cahoots with the federal prosecutors and the F.B.I.? I knew that Gedney was friends with Bart Daniel, the U.S. Attorney. What if he and Daniel had made a deal?

In my imagination, I could hear Gedney's voice: "It's a weak case. I can win it. You know I can win it, Bart. I get Wilkes' money and we'll both get a lot of publicity and then we'll open a law practice together."

This was what I was thinking. This was one of

the crazy thoughts indicative of my state of mind.

At this point, I sat up in bed and told myself to stop it, to calm down. I am innocent. I will be all right. This is America and everything will be fine. I tried to go to sleep, but couldn't.

Around three A.M. I got up and left my guest cottage. I walked to the end of the driveway. The crape myrtles were blooming, and I could smell the sweetness of roses in the front yard. I remembered the first time I had seen Vanderhorst Street. It was in the early 1950s.

We had moved to Winnsboro from Blackstock, South Carolina, because my mother got a job at the mill here. It was called the U.S. Rubber Company. It made tire cord. Those were the days when the structure of tires was made out of fabric, not steel. It was hard work. I think Mama was only making $30 a week. We really couldn't afford rent, so she found us a good situation.

There was a lady named Miss Maggie Douglas who owned a house on Vanderhorst Street, which ran parallel to Main. The house was paintless. It had a rusted tin roof and a chimney that was falling apart. There were cracks between the floorboards and through them you could see chickens nesting under the house. Miss Maggie was an invalid. In lieu of rent, Mama and Robin and I took care of her. We had to give her baths and cook her dinner and sometimes we had to feed her.

I can still remember the morning Miss Maggie died. I was out in the backyard playing. I was five or six years old. Mama came out all distressed and said that Miss Maggie was dead. She took Robin and me into the old lady's room. It was in the summer, and I remember the heat from the day before was still in her room. It smelled like Miss Maggie—very sweet and very sour all at the same time. She was lying in bed on her back and she looked white and still and I touched her hand. It was the coldest flesh I had ever felt.

We called the funeral parlor and they came and got her. I felt sad. She was a woman who had helped us a lot. I had never experienced death before.

But I had other people to look after me. Mrs. McFadden and her daughter Barbara were two of them. They lived in the house next door. When Mama had to work overtime or something, Mrs. McFadden would look after me. She baked me gingerbread cookies and read me stories and let me play on her front porch.

There was also Pearl. She was a black lady who worked for Mrs. McFadden. I loved Pearl. She always knew how to calm me down when I was upset. And she could see into me, too. She had the ability to know if something was wrong. She had lots of children and grandchildren. They were my buddies while I was growing up in Winnsboro. We used to have fun playing on Main Street.

These were happy days, but soon things would start to go wrong. There was one primary reason for this: it was the period Mama started drinking.

Oh, I think she'd had a drink before. I'm not saying she had not, but this was the time when I began to notice that she was losing control of it. She was staying out late at night; she became mercurial and irritable; sometimes she didn't keep her promises.

I've gone back and tried to figure why it happened. Why she became an alcoholic. I understand that research shows that there may be some kind of genetic cause, but there were plenty of other causes in her life. Here she was—a young, beautiful, talented woman—stuck in a dead-end job. It was the reason she left Blackstock at 19. She knew she was talented. She knew she was bright, and she so much wanted to develop and use that talent. She so much wanted to be a success.

But it was 1954 and she was a widow with two little kids and all her dreams were dead. She was lonely. She was sad. She started drinking to kill the pain of it all. I don't blame her for that. She was a wonderful woman, a talented woman, but this drinking problem got worse and worse. I think that she had always been an obsessive, compulsive personality, but the drinking made that behavior more pronounced. I remember one day I went into the kitchen and she was sitting at the table. There were all these pieces of paper in front of her. I'll never forget: she was hunched over, writing with a pencil, her beautiful face all scrunched up and scowling as she scrawled words across a page.

"Mama, what you doing?" I asked.

"Working, honey."

"Working on what?"

"A book."

"Did it fall apart?"

"I'm writing a book, honey. Mama is going to be a writer."

"Why?"

"Well, 'cause that's what I'm going to be."

She went on writing until it was time to go to the mill. She kept working at the book for a few weeks, then she stopped. This was the way she was about everything. She would begin with great intensity, work along and finally give it up, and then she would drink hard and long to make herself forget that she had given it up.

During these periods of drinking, our home descended into complete chaos. There was no order to things, no kept time schedule. Robin and I ate most of our meals at either the Royal Hotel or at Mrs. Gardner's Tourist Home. Our home became a mess. Dishes sat piled up in the sink for days. Leftover food sat in pots on the stove. I tried to clean some, but I was still too young to do it right. That house embarrassed me for many years, though the people inside it did not, particularly my mother.

All my good characteristics had come from her. Time and time again during the ordeal that I was to endure, I would think back to the early days when she provided the warmth and direction of my life.

I still do.

# 4

About ten days after I hired Gedney, he called me to say that Bart Daniel and the federal prosecutors wanted a meeting. I asked what the meeting was about and Gedney said he wasn't sure, but probably they were going to present the evidence they had against me and offer me a deal.

A couple of days later, Gedney, Kenny and I walked from my Columbia office to the Federal Building. It was a hot day. As soon as we walked into the building, we were searched. We then went through a series of doors. I've never seen so many doors in one building in my life. It was like a maze—door after door, and all of them slamming shut behind me. I am convinced that the F.B.I. did all of this deliberately. It made me feel as if I were in prison already—locks and doors and keys and searches.

Finally, we got to a small room. We sat and waited. There was a T.V. in the room and a cassette recorder. I was thinking of Gedney's counsel: "Don't volunteer anything. Don't say anything. These boys are smart and they will use anything you say, anything at all to get you. Just sit and listen and let them talk."

When Bart Daniel and John Barton walked in,

they were solemn, grave, impeccably dressed. Barton did most of the talking. He was the chief prosecutor working for Bart Daniel.

The first thing Barton said was that he wanted to show us the videotapes of me accepting money from Ron Cobb.

My heart was pounding. I was sweating. I had never seen the tapes and despite the fact that I was innocent, I was afraid of them. Had they been doctored? Had words been put in my mouth? Had the tapes been edited to make me look guilty?

Barton put a cassette into the recorder and the tape began to play on the T.V. monitor.

I was surprised. The video was in black and white. The picture was poor quality and the audio was equally bad. You could barely understand what Cobb or I was saying. I was convinced that this was part of the F.B.I. tactics. The grainy texture of the video and the low grumbling of the audio could make anyone look guilty.

Suddenly, I remembered the time I had run into Ron Cobb at a party that Kirk and Rab Finlay threw. They lived at Millwood, the ancestral home of the Hamptons, one of the most prominent families in the history of South Carolina.

It was a perfect setting for such an affair. The Hampton Family (Rab was a Hampton by blood) had been horse lovers for two hundred years. There were tents set up on the manicured grass, servants passing around drinks and all the beautiful people that Columbia society could provide. Others were provided as well. Unknown to the hosts, the F.B.I. had infiltrated the party. In fact, Ron Cobb wore a microphone and tape recorder so that he could get anything he could on everyone he could. I found out that he had taped me at this party. Over the course of the investigation, I discovered that I had been secretly taped a number of times. It made me furious. It reminded me of the KGB.

As I listened and watched the videotape, I was filled with a sense of foreboding. Cobb seemed to be so slick and charming and to be using words so carefully. At the time, I didn't think this. At the time, in fact, I was flattered to be with Cobb in his office. He was a celebrated lobbyist and he had called me, a freshman representative, to help him get his pari-mutuel betting bill through the House. I was convinced that the only reason Cobb would do this was because he must have heard good things about my skills in the legislature. I thought that Cobb wanted to give me a campaign contribution because he respected my abilities to work for legislation in which I believed. It was not at all unusual for a person or a group of people to give a politician a campaign contribution.

The South Carolina Education Association had given me a thousand dollars because they wanted me to be reelected so I could help them fight their battles. At one of my political rallies in Winnsboro, they had announced that I had a perfect record on education and that they were going to contribute to my campaign because they knew that I was loyal to their cause and they needed my help. The money they promised me was not a bribe—it was a contribution. It was the way you got things done.

Anyway, the tape was running and I was

watching Ron Cobb and me in his office. I remember Kenny was sitting on the floor taking notes because the T.V. monitor was low and he wanted to be close to it. Gedney was standing directly behind me.

All of a sudden, we got to the part in the tape where Cobb handed me ten one hundred dollar bills. Right at that point, John Barton stopped the tape and said, "There you are, Wilkes. There you are, taking the money."

I thought: well, yes, there I am taking a campaign contribution, so what?

He did not stop the tape at other points where I was saying things that would show that I knew I was taking a *contribution*—not a bribe. I had said a number of things to indicate that I thought there was nothing abnormal going on.

Then, Barton played the second videotape, and he did exactly the same thing as before. When we got to the place where Cobb was counting out money, Barton froze the tape and said, "See? Got you taking the money a second time."

Well, Gedney, Kenny and I sat there, and Barton and Daniel left. For a while no one said anything. Frankly, I thought the office was probably bugged, so I didn't want to say anything.

After a few seconds, Gedney told me that they would come back and make me an offer. Just as he finished his sentence, Daniel and Barton returned.

Daniel began speaking. He told me that since I had four counts against me, if I were indicted and convicted, that I could get as much as 60 years in prison and seven hundred thousand dollars in fines.

There was silence in the room. I was stunned.

Daniel then said that there were certain guidelines for sentences in the federal court system. He said that the judge in the case would listen carefully to whatever the federal prosecutors asked for in terms of sentencing. He went on to say that he wanted two things from me: to confess that I was guilty and to lend him substantial assistance in convicting other state legislators.

At that point, I couldn't keep quiet anymore.

"Substantial assistance? I don't even know most of the people you're talking about. I didn't socialize with them. I didn't hang out with them at The Town House Hotel. I don't know anything about them."

Gedney gave me a signal to keep quiet.

Bart Daniel smiled and proceeded. He said that if I pleaded guilty and lent him substantial assistance, he would ask the judge to give me a lesser sentence: maybe as little as 18 months and a year on parole.

"18 months? Don't you understand? You're talking about my whole life here: my CPA firm, my reputation, my political career."

Again, Gedney signaled to be quiet.

"Look," Daniel said. "If you plead guilty, we can do a lot to help you. We can go to the Board of Accountancy about your license. We can talk to the judge about sending you to a prison that's easy, a place that's not so bad. There's a lot of things we can do for you."

Daniel looked at me for a moment, then said: "But, if you don't help us, we will go for an upward departure on your sentence. We will make sure you get the maximum number of years and that you spend them in the worst hellhole we can find."

This tough guy approach made me angry. I don't like people getting in my face. I don't like people giving me ultimatums. I also was furious that he had presumed I was guilty and presumed that I was going to plead guilty.

I looked him in the eye and I said: "There are two things I will never do: confess that I'm guilty when I'm not and set somebody else up to go through this kind of hell. I will never do either of these things."

Gedney looked at me and said that I should not close down any of my options. I think that this meeting took place on a Friday. Gedney told Bart that we needed to think about things over the weekend. He said that we needed a copy of the videotapes and the audiotapes and that we needed to review them before we could respond. Gedney also said we needed the transcripts of these tapes—the written words. Ultimately, we didn't get the transcripts of the audiotapes until just before the trial, and I'm convinced there was one reason for this: they would have helped to show my innocence.

At the end of the meeting, Daniel said that he would give me a week to make up my mind and that if he didn't hear from me, they'd come after me with all they had. This turned out to be just another threat, another manipulation, because in the course of events, the prosecutors came to me several times and gave me several more deadlines.

After the meeting, Gedney and Kenny left. I went back to my office and told Bill McDowell what had happened. I said I wasn't sure how to handle things. He gave me some terrific advice. He said to make a ledger sheet—typical and sound accountant thinking. He said to list the debits and the credits. The heading on the sheet would be to plea or not to plea. He said assign a value to all the things on the ledger sheet and then just total them up.

So I drove back to Winnsboro. My mind was boiling with all that was happening to me. I got home and Katherine was there. We made some good pasta and drank wine and made love and I got through another day.

The next morning I went out by the pool and made out my ledger sheet while Katherine baked in the sun.

When I had listed all the debits and credits, it was clear to me that if I pleaded guilty, I would lose everything: my business, my loved ones, my political career, even my self-respect. On the other hand, if I fought, I believed I could win.

A day or two later, I called Gedney and told him this. I told him I would not plead guilty and that I would fight until there was not a breath of air in my lungs or a drop of blood in my body.

After this conversation, I went over to my office. I tried to sit down and do some work. I couldn't concentrate very well. I felt that something awful was going to happen. I wasn't sure what. I needed someone to talk to, so I went to Ken Goode's office, but he wasn't there. I walked over to Main Street and stared at the building that used to house Doctor Buchanan's office. He had been a very important man in my life when I was a boy. If Norman Rockwell had painted a picture of a small-town southern doctor, he would have looked just like Doctor Buchanan. He was average height with silver hair and rosy cheeks and had about him an air of cheerful sophistication and perceptive kindness. He was our family physician for 30 years and he never charged us one penny.

Doug Buchanan was his son. We were friends. One Friday night when we were still kids, Dougie asked his father if he could bring me to supper. His father said sure, and Doug asked what was for supper and his father said hamburgers and hot dogs and Doug said, "Nope, not for my friend, not for Tim. We got to have steaks, Daddy."

"Why do we have to have steaks?"

"Because."

"Oh."

So Doctor Buchanan went out and bought steaks, which was pretty amazing because steak in the 1950s for most people was a delicacy.

The Buchanans lived in a large house that looked like something out of Gone With The Wind. It had columns and porches and was surrounded by magnolias and holly trees.

I got to Doug's around five o'clock that afternoon. Dinner was at six. We ate in their dining room. I had never seen such a beautiful room in my life. There was a long table and glittering silverware and plates. From the center of the room hung a crystal chandelier that threw colored light against the white walls. I felt awkward. Doctor Buchanan and Doug seemed so sure of themselves. They knew exactly how to handle their silverware. Their posture was perfect, and even the way they talked seemed correct—quietly and with a sense of dignity.

I remember that Doctor Buchanan said the blessing. I watched the way they cut up their meat and tried to cut mine the same way. When I finally got a piece of the steak to my mouth, I couldn't believe the taste—it was salty and sweet and peppery and juicy.

"This is wonderful," I said.

"Good," said the Doctor.

"It's the best thing I ever had."

"Glad you like it," Doug said.

"What is it?" I asked.

"Pardon?" said Doctor Buchanan.

"What's this called?"

There was a moment of quiet.

"It's steak," Doug said. "You know—steak."

I looked at him and smiled and kept eating.

Doctor Buchanan told me this story almost 30 years later. It made me a little sad when he told me: that at nine years old I had never even tasted steak. To be poor is hard and lonely and embarrassing, but there is another side to it: if you work hard and make yourself successful, you will find the world full of wonderful things to taste and see and do—simple things that everyone else takes for granted—things like steak.

This was about the time in my life when I got

my first job. I think I was nine years old. I was too young to work; that is, people weren't supposed to hire me, but they knew my family needed the money. I went to Tommy Tolbert's pool hall on Main Street and asked if they had anything I could do. Tommy handed me a broom and said to sweep the place out.

It was one of the dirtiest, nastiest places I had ever been in. There was mud and sawdust and cigarette butts and black wads of chewing tobacco all over the floor. The bathroom didn't even have a door. It had a kind of partition with a hole cut in it so if you were sitting down you could watch and make sure nobody moved the balls on your table.

One afternoon, I had been working for about two hours in the pool hall. I had swept and scrubbed the floor and was getting ready to haul out a load of trash when the manager asked me to come behind the bar. When I got back there, he was kneeling down in front of a drawer. I remember his grey hair was thick and matted. He had not washed it in a while and it smelled sour. He motioned me closer to the drawer.

"Want to see something really purdy?"

"What is it?"

"Want to feel it? It ain't nothing like you ever felt before?"

I was nervous. I felt that he wanted me to do something that was wrong.

He pulled open the drawer and grabbed my hand and stuck it inside.

I tried to break free, but couldn't and so I let him guide my hand across the surface.

"How's that feel, boy?"

"Alright."

"Alright. Hell, I bet you never felt anything like that in your life. Know what it is?"

I broke my hand from his grip and looked at him. I didn't like anybody putting their hands on me.

"It's pure, genuine, made-in-China silk."

With that, the old man took out the robe from the drawer. It was white. He slipped it over his clothes and then got the white, cone hat and mask and pulled it over his head. Across the top of his eyes "KKK" was stitched in bright red letters. He stuck his hands on his hips and laughed and said:

"What do you think?"

"It doesn't scare me."

"It ain't s'posed to scare you. It's s'posed to scare niggers."

I knew about the Ku Klux Klan. I had heard my family talk about them.

"Cowards and scoundrels," I said. "The only kind of people who put on those robes are cowards and scoundrels."

There was silence, and then he tore off the hood. His face was red and his brown eyes bulged from his head.

"Better mind what you say, boy."

"My Mama told me about the KKK." I thought he was going to hit me, but I refused to move and I refused to back down from my stand.

After a while, he just walked away.

This recollection made me smile. For whatever reason, all the uncertainty about my future was focusing my eyes back upon my past. I drew strength from it.

# 5

Early in the morning of August 3, 1990 I awoke and put on my blue jeans and worked in my rose garden. By the time I had sprayed all of the bushes, the newspaper came. The sting now had a name. The Feds dubbed it Operation Lost Trust. I read the story on the front page.

This story worried me about as much as the first one which broke on July 18. The very idea that Congressmen Arthur Ravenel and Floyd Spence had said that the sting was going to be a "blockbuster" and that it would send shock waves throughout the nation filled me with trepidation.

Exactly how big was the operation? I knew that all the disclosure records had been seized for both the South Carolina House and the Senate, but I thought that perhaps it was because the F.B.I. was just trying to do their job effectively. Maybe I was wrong. Maybe scores of senators and representatives were about to be indicted. Originally, I felt that maybe three or four people would go down and then the rest would be slapped with a warning and a fine. Now that idea changed. Whatever was going to happen would be much bigger than I had anticipated.

After a few weeks, the initial shock of the investigation and the publicity began to wear off. I tried to get back to a normal routine, though I was still rather uncomfortable around people, particularly people I didn't know. One of the things that kept me going was the certainty of my innocence. Still, my self-esteem was helped quite a lot when the superintendent of schools called and asked if I would deliver the graduation address for the summer school class of Fairfield Central High School. I readily accepted, and this invitation helped to further construct my cocoon of innocence. I was thinking: see, even school teachers know you're innocent. If they thought you were guilty, they wouldn't have you speaking to young people. It is obvious to everyone that you are an innocent man. So be calm. All this will blow over.

Little did I know, it had just begun.

Despite all of Katherine's capriciousness, I found myself more and more dependent upon her. I was deeply in love, but it was a difficult relationship. We fought often. Many times when I should have been focusing on a particular legal problem, something would come up between Katherine and me and all I could do was think about her. Between us there was ecstasy and agony and because of this seesaw relationship, I often was distracted from what the F.B.I. wanted to do to me. At the time, I wanted Katherine to be supportive—which she sometimes was—but looking back, I can see that all of the fighting and lovemaking and breakups and reunions were good therapy for me.

The guy I could not have done without was Kenny Goode. While I was trying to get through the investigation (which I was convinced would exonerate me of all wrongdoing) I went to Kenny's office two to three times a day. My office sits right behind his, and I literally wore a path beneath the walnut trees and through the crape myrtles to his door.

Kenny's office is a place that should appear on the Andy Griffith show. It is the epitome of what a small-town lawyer's office should be. It sits in a white house on Main Street. It has tall ceilings and is cluttered with collections of things: an aggregation of canes and walking sticks, a tiger skin rug, shelves full of old bottles, old dental equipment, rows of books and arrowheads and tomahawks and drums; there are parts of things everywhere—parts of cars and trucks and boats and guns. The walls are cluttered with pictures and portraits of his wife and kids; circus posters and political posters and gaudy advertisements. In a way, Kenny Goode's office is like a small museum.

I would go in and pour out my soul to him, ask endless questions, pose endless scenarios of what might happen, what could happen, what possibly would happen. Through it all, Kenny would sit and listen and counsel and advise—and I wasn't paying him a penny.

Kenny and I had met in high school. We came from similar economic backgrounds, which is to say that we were both of very modest means. One difference was that he had (and has) a wonderful mother and father who looked after and encouraged him. We spent a lot of good times in high school, then went off to college and began to build our careers.

Years later, we came back to Winnsboro and became close once again. We saw each other almost every day and became involved in one another's lives—both business and personal. We were always buying each other's houses or furniture or paintings. I remember one purchase in particular. Ken owned a Mercedes and a Porsche that he wanted to sell. I drove them both over a two-week period, but could not make up my mind. One night, he called and said he needed to know which one I wanted. I had drunk a couple glasses of wine, so I said, "Hell, I'll buy them both." The next morning he appeared at my door with the keys to the two cars and a bill of sale and asked me for $50,000. We laughed and I bought the cars.

Since I couldn't sleep well at night, I spent a lot of time reading. I had graduated from the University of South Carolina with a degree in English. Even though I had to work a number of jobs to get through school, I loved studying literature. I was mesmerized by the haunting images of Melville and Conrad, and utterly beguiled by the simplicity of Hemingway, the convolutions of Faulkner and the lyrical genius of Thomas Wolfe. All of these writers took up residence in my heart and helped to shape my view of the world.

I think it was beneficial to have nourished myself with a sense of poetry before I entered the corporate world. There is no poetry there, only the logic of the bottom line.

My first job with a corporation came when I started to work for the Phillip Morris Company. It was a huge business. It sold tobacco on every continent in the world, and I was thrilled to get on with them as a salesman.

Phillip Morris was very organized in its training of young salesmen. They sent me to Richmond and then New York. They filmed me as I practiced selling the product to various fictional customers. I learned a great deal from this course of study.

When I got in the field, I was a fireball. I worked long days. I learned how to turn on something in myself when I met a customer. It was like flipping a switch. I learned that when armed with a smile and charm and a good product, the customer couldn't say no. Soon I became a good salesman. Phillip Morris then offered me a regional manager's job. They wanted me to move to Atlanta. I was flattered by the offer, but I knew I couldn't go. I had to look after Mama. I couldn't live with myself if I didn't. This, of course, was a mistake in terms of business. It was not a mistake, in terms of the human heart, and I still had the sensitivity of Thomas Wolfe and James Agee stored up in my bones. Phillip Morris was not pleased, but they kept me on. In fact, they paid for me to start working on my MBA at the University. While I was working at Phillip Morris and going to school, I also had part-time jobs at an accounting firm and selling real estate.

In the middle of all this work, I got a call one day that Mama was sick. I immediately called my girlfriend and the two of us drove to Winnsboro.

Mama looked terrible. She was an awful orange-yellow color and her stomach was hugely swollen. There was a smell in her room, the smell of death. I knew I had to do something, say something. I was being a salesman, yet again. I had to sell Mama on staying alive. That very evening in her hot, sticky bedroom on Vanderhorst Street, I came up with the best idea I could summon.

"Mama, Pat and I have a little announcement to make."

She turned her face in my direction, but didn't say anything.

"We want to get married. We've just made the decision. So you need to get well quick and get out of that bed. There's a thousand things to do. Announcements, parties and all the rest of it. We need you now more than ever."

For the first time that day, Mama smiled.

In two weeks, she was out of bed and helping to plan the wedding. From the day she left her hospital bed, until the day of her death, she never drank or smoked again. And she did it cold turkey. Pat and I were married a few months later. Unfortunately, this marriage did not last, nor did a later one.

# 6

During late August of 1990, I tried to meet with my clients and tried to help the people of Fairfield County as their representative. But some days I could not concentrate and would just go home and pace my backyard.

I remember one day in particular I was walking back and forth wondering if I could overcome whatever was lying ahead of me and for some reason I recalled an event that occurred when I was young.

Mama had been working at the mill for years and still wasn't making very much money. I remember when it got close to payday, food got pretty slim. We ate a lot of grits and salmon cakes. Sometimes we ate it three or four days in a row. I didn't complain because I knew Mama was having a hard time. She was drinking more now. She was single and pretty and occasionally she had dates. It was hard for me to deal with. I didn't know what was going on, but I knew that it made me feel angry and threatened. There was one incident in particular that left an impression. It had to do with my Uncle George.

George Brown was my uncle by marriage. He had married my mother's sister, Louise. While Aunt

Louise was alive, everything was all right. She and Uncle George would come over and drink with Mama and that was fine. The trouble started when Aunt Louise died. A week or two after her death, George arrived at the house, bringing whiskey, getting Mama drunk. I didn't like it. At the very least, I thought that Uncle George shouldn't be carrying liquor into our house, that he should know it was bad for Mama. But there was something else going on between them—something dark, and I hated it.

One night, George was being obnoxious as usual. He was a retired army sergeant and he spoke loudly and his language was vulgar. I still remember how he looked: he was short and hairy and wore a cowboy hat and cowboy boots and smoked an odious cigar. He was drunk. The drunker he got, the more I worried, so I started following Mama and him all over the house. They'd go to the living room; I'd go to the living room. They'd go to the back porch; I'd go to the back porch. This continued for a while and then George got up and disappeared. He came back in a moment and told me to come into the next room with him.

I can still smell the stench of his cigar and see the patches of black fur on the back of his arms and the back of his neck. When he turned around, he pulled a .45 pistol from out of his pants and pointed it right between my eyes.

"What's your problem, kid?"

The barrel of that .45 looked huge. I could smell the linseed oil on it.

"I ain't got a problem."

"Why you been following me around?"

"Why are you here? Why are you in my house?"

"I'm having a good time."

"It's not right. None of it's right. You know it's not."

George stuck the muzzle of the pistol against my forehead.

"I'll tell you what, Junior. We're having the changing of the guard in this house. You understand? We're having the changing of the guard and you better watch your damn step or you might get your head blown clean, damn off."

At that point, I pushed the gun from my face and ran for my room.

I didn't run because I was scared. I ran to even things up a little bit. I went into my room and got my baseball bat. Instantly, I knew what to do. George had something that he loved more than booze and women. It was sitting out front on Vanderhorst Street: a brand new black Buick.

I ran straight to the car and started working it over with the bat. I smashed everything I could get to: windows, taillights, mirrors. Glass flew everywhere and the sound of it shattering brought George running outside carrying his pistol.

"You little sonofabitch! What are you doing?"

"You get out of here, George."

"My car. What did you do to my car?"

He stopped and looked at me and I got a good grip on the bat. About that time, Mrs. Harmon and Mrs. McFadden turned on the porch light and walked outside. When he saw them, he left. I watched the one taillight disappear into the darkness and we never saw him again.

When I returned from this memory, I felt a little better. I had faced difficult odds all my life and I had always prevailed. I sat down on my stone wall and looked at my yard.

It was high summer. Everything was green: the pecan trees and the walnuts, the rose bushes and the tea olives—all were brilliant green and so full of life and strength, and yet when I would look at them, I felt this awful sense of dread sometimes. It would creep up and steal into me, this terrible feeling that something was going to happen, something that I could not control, and then I would lose all the greenness and all the life and begin to feel again the awful cold, the cold I had felt the very first day, and in the last of August I would shiver like a man who has felt the coming of winter, the first bleak winds of the lightless days.

Then on September 28 it happened—the catastrophe that I had been dreading.

# 7

It was an explosion, or perhaps more accurately an implosion. The entire state government and all its miscellaneous and variegated parts had suddenly collapsed, burying all those who had worked in public service, inundating all those who had sought political life, entangling and ensnarling and fouling all those who had represented the people of South Carolina for 30 years.

I was stunned. I read story after story about this lawmaker receiving money and that one asking for gifts and this one pleading for special favors. Many of these men I knew. I had served with them, worked with them, fought their fights and celebrated their victories and endured their defeats. I was completely shocked at what I was finding out, and as the revelations continued, I began to feel a growing sense of shame and humiliation. These were supposed to be the servants, the representatives of the people of South Carolina. They had been given the faith and trust of millions, and what had they done with it? They had stained the trust of all those who had believed in them.

I was sick with shame. Why would these men have done this? Why would they have sold their votes?

For money? How much money—a few thousand dollars? Had they destroyed themselves and their careers and the honor of the General Assembly for a few thousand bucks?

I was devastated; but more than this, I began to be afraid. My picture, my name, was printed in bold letters and sat right alongside all the others. What would people think of me? They would think I was guilty, a crook like the others. I wasn't. I was innocent, but I knew that people would not see it this way. They would only see my name and my face and would say, "Yeah, Tim Wilkes, he's one of them. There ain't no doubt."

The entire climate in the state had changed. Before there was anxiety, but now there was fear. It ate at me night and day. I felt as though I were on the edge of an abyss and that any moment someone was going to come along and push me into the roiling mess below.

There was no sleep for me at night. All I could do was watch TV and pace around the house, pace around the yard, pace up and down the streets. Would they indict me? Would someone appear at my door in the middle of the night and stick a summons in my hand?

I spent night after night at Barbara Harmon's. I sought her wisdom, her reassurance and her kindness. I badgered Gedney Howe with questions and pummeled Kenny Goode with possible scenarios of destruction.

One night I slept a little and had a terrible vision. I saw a great, black train beginning to move down the tracks. I was standing at the other end and the black locomotive of the F.B.I. was churning straight for me.

I was eaten up with the news and newspapers and news specials and magazine stories and articles and promos and sidebars. I almost became the news, and the only way I could endure it at night was to drink, to open the long smooth bottles and swallow as if I could swallow the whole sting, swallow as if I could drink down the whole misery of it until there was nothing left but a vapor, a smell, a hint of all the burning pain, and then I would sleep fitfully and awfully until the light brought me back to the darkness of my days.

Some time in late September of 1990, I began to pull myself back together. I made myself start eating better. I spent a lot of time with Katherine and tried to get out with her a bit. I tried to return to some sense of normalcy. I got up at five A.M., whether I had slept or not. I worked out on the heavy bag, lifted a few weights, turned on my Krups coffee maker and got in the jacuzzi.

Slowly, I restored a sense of balance in my life. I was talking to Gedney Howe often.

I had paid Gedney the fifty-thousand-dollar fee, which pretty much drained me of cash. He was counseling me to stay out of the public eye, to be conservative, to be quiet.

"You got to keep your ass out of bars," Gedney said.

"I like bars. They help me forget."

"Well, stay out of them, and don't be seen with the young blonds."

"I like young blonds."

"Now look, Wilkes, you got to be low profile

and quiet. You are being watched and are probably under police surveillance. The last thing in the world you need is to have people take notice of you. Stay at home and stay out of the newspaper and don't cause me trouble."

"Hey, listen, damn it, I just paid you fifty thousand dollars. If I want to cause you some trouble, I'll cause you some trouble."

"You want your money back?"

"Yeah."

"You'll get it tomorrow."

He slammed down the phone. So did I. The next day, we talked again and made up. This was the way things would be between Gedney and me throughout the next ten months. He wouldn't let me live my life the way I wanted and wouldn't tell me the things I wanted to hear. He had given good advice, but I was too hardheaded and arrogant to take it.

At this point, there were news stories in the media every day about the sting. I was doing my best to get used to it. Gedney had told me that Bart Daniel was trying his strongest cases first. He said that it was possible that if Daniel lost a couple that the F.B.I. would not indict me. I was clinging to that possibility, but it seemed that every time I allowed myself a little hope, yet another series of indictments came down.

In addition, more and more was coming out about Ron Cobb. I couldn't believe what I read. There seemed to be a real possibility that Cobb wanted his wife dead? How could the F.B.I. use such a man? He was a drug dealer. He was an adulterer. He was a thief having stolen from his own spouse—if what she was saying was true.

This caused me to see the F.B.I. and Bart Daniel in a new light. They would use anyone and do anything in order to get what they wanted. It didn't matter to them if Cobb was a villain, they simply wanted to nail people to the wall, and if they had to cozy-up-to, buy, support, congratulate and cosset a man like Cobb, they would do it.

# 8

I hit a new low. If the F.B.I. would go to these lengths, what possible chance did I have against them?

In the middle of all this uncertainty and anxiety, I did something which only made matters worse. Katherine and I had had one of our many fights and she had moved out of my home. A friend called and asked me to go to a University of South Carolina football game. I was feeling miserable, but I went. If Katherine had been with me, I wouldn't have driven.

The Gamecocks were losing badly and I didn't want to stay and see the end of it, so I left. I had been drinking, and I shouldn't have gotten into my car, but I thought I could handle it. On the way home, I was pulled. The officer put me through a few tests and I passed them all, but he was not impressed, so he took me in for the Breathalyzer. I was horrified. I thought: great Tim, here you go and do something foolish like this. What's the matter with you? Do you want to be indicted? Are you trying to destroy yourself?

I remember at one point I said to the patrolman, "Can't you loosen these cuffs? My wrists are bleeding."

He looked at me and didn't smile and said:

"They ain't supposed to be comfortable, Mister Wilkes."

He took me down to the county jail in Columbia. I took the Breathalyzer and failed. Before I was locked up, the guard allowed me one phone call and I got to Kenny.

"What?"

"I'm in jail. D.U.I."

"Jesus, Tim."

"What do I do?"

"Don't take a blood test."

"Okay."

"Did you take the Breathalyzer?"

"Yeah."

"What'd it read?"

"I don't know."

"Doesn't matter. I know those machines inside and out."

"Kenny, what the hell have I done?"

"Take it easy. I'll have you out in four or five hours."

I was fingerprinted. My photograph was taken. They put me in a large cell, full of men. There must have been 30. It was a horrible place. The floor was cement and a mess. It was covered with urine and vomit and spilt food and drink. There was the stink of this and there was the salty, sour odor of men imprisoned. There was another smell that was more subtle, but also more powerful. It was the smell of steel. The cold, bright smell of the unbreakable, uncuttable, unrelenting metal that surrounded me and the others.

I couldn't sit still. I paced back and forth. The

place was like something out of a movie. Men of every kind were here: men in silk suits and men in blue jeans with no shirts; men in uniforms and men in cut-off shorts; men with coiffed hair and pinky rings and men with skin heads and tattoos.

Now and again wives would appear and walk to the edge of the bars to talk to their husbands. Occasionally, other family members would show up. It was a place of sorrow, a den of remorse and regret and sadness that ran from the deepest channels of the heart. And looking at all of it and feeling all of it, I thought: I can't stand this. Is this what prison is like? I simply cannot bear this. I feel like some kind of animal. I have no privacy, no space, no silence. I remembered what Gedney told me that a judge could give me—if I was indicted; if I was convicted—12 years, no parole. How could I stay in a place like this for 12 years? It was nearly impossible to endure for five or six hours. I couldn't stand it for 12 whole years.

I sat down in a corner. For a while I didn't think about anything. And then I thought about everything.

None of us was far away from this. Oh, we all thought we were. We all thought we had good jobs, and good health, and we were sitting pretty, and nothing like this could ever happen to us, but we were wrong.

I was thinking clearly now, so clearly that it was almost like a vision. Everyone is only one step away, one speeding ticket away, one temper tantrum, one lost job away from ending up here. Let's say you've bitten off more than you can chew. You bought a big home and a fancy sports car and you can't make the payments, so you take a little money from your company; you end up here. Or you have too much to drink and get in a fight with an in-law and punch the guy out; you end up here. Everyone could end up here with just one mistake, with one serious loss of control.

I spent the rest of the day considering how close to disaster we all are. We take so many things for granted, particularly our freedom. Around seven o'clock, Kenny made the arrangements and they let me out.

When I got back home, it was another sleepless night, but the one thing that came out of it was that no matter how hard I had to fight or what it cost me, I would never allow myself to go to prison. I was completely and adamantly determined that if I was indicted, I would fight and I would win.

In January of 1991, the General Assembly went back into session. When I returned to the great chamber of the State House, I noticed that some of my colleagues treated me differently. There was a coolness and distance. It bothered me a great deal, but I tried to keep myself busy with business and tried to not think about it. At this point, the sting was the biggest news story in the state. Lobbyists and legislators were rolling over and ratting on each other. It was a skin game. Everybody was trying to save his own hide. There was paranoia. Everyone was suspicious of everyone else. No politician would talk on the telephone for fear it was tapped. No one would go near a reporter for fear they would be connected to Lost Trust. Ron Cobb was the plague bacillus and he had brought this terrible disease into the life of the entire political structure of South Carolina.

At night, I was still going out to bars and drinking hard. Katherine and I spent a lot of time together. One day she came to the House chamber and brought a cousin of hers. It happened to be one of the periods when we were getting along fairly well. Katherine's cousin was going to Harvard Law School and I decided it was worth mentioning to the House, so I introduced both of them. There was polite applause. This is not so unusual a thing to do. A lot of legislators introduce guests. An hour later, Gedney called me.

"What the hell are you doing, Wilkes?"

"What do you mean?"

"I told you to keep a low profile. I told you not to attract attention to your asinine self, and what did you go and do?"

"I didn't do anything."

"You're showing your ass with your blond girlfriends in the State House. Do you know how that looks? Do you know what everyone is thinking?"

This made me think that Gedney had spies in the State House. It made me suspicious of him. I felt like I was being watched by everybody: the media, the F.B.I., my own lawyer.

Gedney continued, "It looks like, well, here I am friends, being investigated by the F.B.I., but I don't give a shit. I'm cool Tim. I got two blonds on my arm and I'm putting them in your face."

"You know what, Gedney? You ought to loosen up a little bit. You ought to get a couple of blonds yourself."

"Wilkes, I'm tired of having to put up with all your crazy, sophomoric, redneck antics."

"And I'm damned sick and tired of dealing with your pseudo-aristocratic, antiquated code of ethics."

"You can go to hell."

"I'll see you there."

We hung up the phone simultaneously.

I figured that was the end. I could not stand someone constantly telling me what I should and shouldn't do. Gedney couldn't abide someone disagreeing with him and not taking his advice.

Later that evening, I called Kenny and told him that I wanted to fire Gedney, and he said to sleep on it.

"I don't want to sleep on it. He is an arrogant sonofabitch and I want him off the case."

"He's the best lawyer in the state."

"Other than you."

"Well, of course."

"I'll sleep on it."

I slept as best I could, and then got up the next day and decided to go with Kenny's advice. I called Gedney, apologized and we got back on track. This was hard for me to do. I was not used to having someone direct my life. Freedom had been one of the most important things for me, and now I was having to surrender my will to someone else.

The black, steaming locomotive of the F.B.I. kept right on rolling down the tracks. Jack Rogers, one of the most colorful, intelligent and powerful men in state politics, was indicted in early January.

A few days after the indictment of Representative John I. "Jack" Rogers, Senator Jack Lindsay died. Everyone knew he was in the hospital, but no one thought that he would die. I was shaken. I was also sure that the sting had killed the distinguished senator as much as anything else.

Jack Lindsay had been the most powerful man in the South Carolina Legislature for a generation. He was intelligent and cunning and ruthless. For years, he had almost single-handedly written the State Budget. He knew South Carolina State Law as well as any judge and he knew how to get a bill through the Senate without having one point of it questioned or debated. He understood the human heart and knew how to charm, manipulate or goad anyone into doing anything. He was the best orator in the General Assembly, combining theatrics with a quick and ready wit. He was the kind of man who would cut your heart out in a debate and at the end of it, throw his arm around you and smile so that you found yourself liking, perhaps even admiring, him. I had admired him for years, not only because of his various talents, but also because he was devoted to the people of Marlboro County and all of South Carolina.

His hounding by the U.S. Attorney made me furious. Didn't they have any sense of ethics at all? Or if that wasn't the question, didn't they have the smallest bit of compassion for a distinguished South Carolinian who was obviously in his last days? I wondered what drove this juggernaut. Oh, yes, there was no doubt that corruption was rife in the state government, that some legislators had sold their souls for money and favors, but it was becoming clear to me that there were others who had sold their souls. One of them was U.S. Attorney Bart Daniel.

# 9

For some reason that I'm not completely aware of, Jack Lindsay's death made me summon up the death of my mother.

In 1978, she had come down with cancer of the mouth. She went through radiation and chemotherapy for a year and we thought she was okay.

It was around this time that I built her a house on a pond in Fairfield County. It was a simple house on a few acres of land, but she loved it.

One Sunday, we were at the pond house watching a football game. She asked me to feel her head, that she had these lumps on her head. There were several, and they were soft. I was horrified. I knew what it was, but I tried to act calm. I told her we would go to the doctor and get it checked out.

She went through a battery of tests again, and all of my fears proved true: it was cancer and it was in her brain and throughout the rest of her body.

The whole process started over again. The chemotherapy and the radiation. Mama began to lose her beautiful hair. Her weight dropped suddenly. I moved to Winnsboro and into the small house on the pond so that I could take care of her. I was completely determined that we were going to beat this thing. I cooked for her and bathed her and made sure that she was taking her medicines on time.

One day, we were coming back from her treatments at the hospital and Mama was having trouble getting out of the car. I helped her out, but then she couldn't walk from the car to the house.

"Honey, I think you're going to have to carry me," she said.

"No. You walk. You've got the strength."

"Tim, I'm too weak."

"Come on."

She took a few steps and then began to fall and I caught her.

"I want you to try it again. You've got to do it, Mama. You can't stop walking. If you stop walking, you can't make it. Come on. Try, just try. One foot in front of the other. You can do it, I know you can. Please try, please, please."

But she wouldn't walk, and so I picked her up in my arms, and I was crying and she was crying. I said to myself that it was the end, that this was the end of her if she couldn't even walk.

I remember holding her in my arms and walking under the pine trees towards the house and hearing the spring peepers crying in the trees and feeling the first warmth of spring and thinking: she's dying, everything is coming to life, and I'm carrying her like she used to carry me, and she's dying, right this very minute, right this second, in my arms, and there's nothing I can do, nothing at all.

Even now, I feel guilty about this, about trying

to make her walk. I did it not to be tough, but because I wanted her to win so desperately, but I feel bad about it because she was doing all she could and I was asking for more.

Still her struggle went on.

I slept in the small bedroom next to her. The cancer crept into her brain until she was not able to talk. She would communicate with me by knocking on the wall at night. One knock was the bathroom, two was water or food, three was the worst. This was what I dreaded more than anything. Three was I'm hurting, come in and sit by me, Timmy, come on and hold my hand in the dark until the pain goes away.

Finally, Mama became so ill I had to put her in Richland Memorial Hospital in Columbia. They kept her as long as the Medicare lasted, then said that she had to move on. That's what the government does: once they determine that there's no more they can do for you, that you're going to die, they tell you to get out. So I took her to nearby Baptist Hospital and went through the same process and the same bureaucratic rules applied and they kicked her out of there. Finally, I brought her back to Winnsboro and put her in Fairfield County Hospital. Doctor Buchanan came to our aid. He simply gave instructions that Mama was staying there as long as she needed to and damn the government and Medicare and damn the rules.

Mrs. Harmon, Mrs. McFadden and I took shifts staying with Mama. One night, I went home about two o'clock and Mrs. Harmon called and told me I needed to come to the hospital. When I got there, she told me that Mama had died. I stood for a moment and closed my eyes, then I went into the room and said goodbye to the woman around whom I had built my life.

I was alone. I have never felt more alone in my life. I began to realize something. I saw that my whole life until this point (I was almost 30 years old) had been devoted to my mother. All my life and all my labors had been dedicated to her. What was I supposed to do now? Who or what was to come first now?

That same feeling of being lost had returned again with the F.B.I. sting. Most of the time I could beat it, I could work myself out of it, but there were some days when I surrendered to an ineluctable sense of gloom. The day Jack Lindsay died was one of those times.

As soon as these new charges had been sent down on February 21, 1991, Bart Daniel was on the phone to Gedney Howe. The question was the same as he had asked before: Didn't Wilkes want to lend substantial assistance? Didn't Wilkes want to plead guilty? Gedney called and asked me. It was his duty to do so. My answer was the same as it had always been: No.

It seemed that every month or so more and more people were being implicated. Bart Daniel was knocking them down right and left. So far he had not lost a case. It was all I could do to keep going, to tend to my responsibilities in the legislature and work in my CPA firm. At night, in order to escape the tension, I went out to bars with Katherine. Most of the time things went well, but there was one evening when I thought both of us might end up in jail.

After I had found out about the fourth set of charges, I went into another depression. It was on a Friday and I called Katherine and told her that I needed to see her. She said she had other plans, that she wanted to go drinking with the girls. Her refusal to see me made me feel even worse. I couldn't be alone that night, so I called Russell Munn. He and his girlfriend, Harriett, met me at Pug's, a favorite bar of mine located in the Five Points part of Columbia.

We sat down in a booth. Just after we had gotten our first drink, Jane Williams walked into the bar. She was an old girlfriend of mine.

"Where's the blond bomber?" she asked, looking at me.

"Drinking with the girls."

"Mind if I sit?"

Jane Williams slid beside me and we talked about the sting.

After while, Russell and Harriett left.

Jane Williams and I ordered another round. Then Katherine walked in. I knew there was going to be trouble. She went straight up to Jane Williams and asked her to leave. Jane refused. With a smile and a flourish, Katherine grabbed her by the wrist and pulled her from the booth. Jane sprawled on the floor, her skirt rising to reveal a pair of black garters with sequins. When Jane got to her feet, Katherine slapped her so hard that both of Jane's earrings shot off her head.

I was thinking: Great. Gedney says to keep a low profile and here I am in the middle of this. I made for the door and Katherine went after me. We argued briefly and I headed to Winnsboro and home.

On March 2, 1991, two more men were nailed.

I was completely distraught. Would I or would I not be indicted? How many bullets were left in the federal gun? Was one for me?

I was calling Gedney all the time.

"Gedney, what's going on?"

"I don't know."

"I'm paying you 50k and you don't know?"

At this point, an old friend came to me and said that he knew a source at the F.B.I. at the top of this investigation. I can't reveal my friend's name, so I'll call him Deep. He said that he had been told that there wasn't sufficient evidence to indict me. Deep's source at the F.B.I. said: "If the U.S. Attorney tries Tim's case, he'll end up shooting his own dick off."

I was so excited that Deep and I went out and partied. I wasn't going to be indicted. Everything was going to work out.

I told Gedney what I had heard and he said Bart Daniel would have the last word. I said that my source was unimpeachable and that it was certain that I was off the hook.

Gedney said he was not certain of anything. A couple of days later, Gedney called back to say it was possible that they might not indict me, but a day later called to say that things had changed again and the indictment would come down. I was bleary and bewildered and completely confused.

# 10

The next day Gedney and I spoke again.

"I had a phone call," Gedney said.

"And?"

"They're going to indict you—I think."

"No, they're not. I've got a source—"

"I don't give a damn about your source. It is Bart Daniel's decision and it looks like he's going for you. Get ready."

It haunted me all night long, this conversation. Lying in bed, I thought about how unfair the whole federal court system is. If the government believes that you are guilty of a crime, they have unlimited resources to come after you. Their most powerful tool is the F.B.I., whose agents are trained at Quantico, Virginia, in methods of interrogation, manipulation and surveillance. Once the F.B.I. conducts their investigation, they take it and present whatever they have found to the grand jury. Unfortunately, you cannot rebut any charges made against you by the F.B.I. before the grand jury with your lawyer present. It is against the rules. After the grand jury reviews the uncontested evidence, they almost always return what is called a True Bill. This is a legal term that means that the grand jury believes there is enough evidence to produce a guilty verdict. Once the True Bill is returned, the federal prosecutors then move for an indictment. This is tantamount to a conviction in many people's mind.

Through this whole process, you can say or do nothing. You must only listen and wait. You cannot protest in any way.

On another night, I drank a half gallon of cheap, white wine. I sat in my jacuzzi and boiled myself pink and the thoughts rattled through my mind: how had this happened to me? Why had this happened to me? All of my life I had been punctilious about ethics. I had prided myself on being ethically correct. Yes, I might drink too much, and yes, I might like the ladies a whole lot, but about honesty and integrity in business, I was most careful and most certain. As a certified public accountant, there were a million times I could have shaved a little bit here and nibbled a little bit there, but I never had. Honesty was the whole basis of my life and my business.

I remembered one event in particular. There was a client of mine, a man in Winnsboro I had known for years. I did his taxes and helped to look after his small business. He died one day, suddenly. He had no family and only a few friends. I was appointed by the Probate Court to take care of his financial matters. He lived in a hovel in a poor part of Winnsboro. I went over. The house was dirty. It was littered with dirty clothes and worthless furniture. The place stank of rotten food. I cleaned things up as best I could and found the papers I needed. I went outside and opened his car, sifting through the glove compartment. In the back seat, I found a paper bag. When I opened it, I discovered money—a lot of money.

I sat in the back seat of the old and battered Nash Rambler and counted it. It came to over five thousand dollars in tens and twenties. I took it back into the house and called Kenny Goode. I told him where I had found it.

"What do I do?"

"How many relatives does he have?"

"None—that I know of."

"Well, then, that's 2,500 dollars for you and 2,500 dollars for me."

We both laughed!

"Come on, Kenny."

"I'm just kidding. We need to tell a judge. Did he have a lawyer?"

He didn't, but we took the money to Probate Court and, after a few weeks, we did find a distant relative. The money was forwarded to her.

If I had been dishonest, it would have been easy to keep this little windfall, but it's not my way. It never has been, and it never will be.

On May 23, 1991 at eleven A.M., the legislature was in session. I was sitting at my desk reading some legislation when the Assistant Sergeant-at-Arms came up to me. His name was Jimmy Walters. We were friends. He came over and quietly tapped me on the shoulder.

"Tim, you need to leave."

"What?"

"You need to just get up and leave right now."

"Jimmy, what's this about?"

"Get your things. Be real quiet."

I knew Jimmy was my friend, and I knew he wouldn't be giving me this warning unless something terrible was about to happen, so I got up and left. I called Katherine and told her to meet me at her apartment. What we had feared for so long was about to happen.

When we got there, I turned on the midday report and there it was: "Representative Tim Wilkes has just been indicted by the U.S. Attorney. One more state legislator has fallen in Operation Lost Trust."

I stayed with Katherine for a while, then I went home by myself. I was stunned by the indictment. Maybe I should not have been, but I was. For months, I had wrapped myself up in the knowledge of my own innocence. I had said to myself time and time again—I am innocent, and because I am innocent, nothing bad will happen to me. I will not be indicted. And now it had happened. I pulled the drapes and turned off the phone. I started pouring wine and sat in the dark and tried to figure what to do.

I gave up on the wine early and moved on to Absolut and soda. I gathered two or three televisions and put them in one room. I watched the six o'clock news and the seven and eleven o'clock reports on as many local channels as I could. It was all the same: Representative Wilkes is indicted. Each report I saw was like a blow, like someone was taking a hammer and beating me in the head. I had a terrible sensation of drowning, that I was going under this black tide, that I couldn't get my breath. It reminded me of a near catastrophe in Hawaii.

I had been surfing hard all day above a hidden reef. Suddenly, a wave knocked me under and somehow I caught the board leash in the coral. I couldn't get up. I was caught below the surface, and sucking in cold saltwater and sand, and I couldn't get up. I thought it was over. I thought it was the end, until I finally broke free.

It was the way I felt now—that I was sucking down all this terribly cold stuff, that I was completely alone, that I was going to die and there was no one to help me.

At some point, I passed out.

The next morning was black. It was as if the blackness started in my head and spread out into everything else. It bled into my coffee and into the jacuzzi and even permeated the sunlight itself, even went into the faces of my roses. I was black and the world was black and there was nothing that did not have blackness in it.

Slowly though, something else began building in me—a kind of angry determination. It took a while. I went to the office and started making notes. I thought about what I had faced in my life and what I had overcome.

I called Gedney and Kenny and they said to go over my day timer and all my records—to relive everything since the day I had met Ron Cobb.

By afternoon, I had scribbled almost a hundred pages: ideas of defense, of attack, memories about my mother, about my father's medals, and my first job, and boxing. I wrote image after image and many things did not connect, but out of it came one primary feeling: I would not give up. I would collect all that I was, all that I had been and would be. I would bring everything together in myself, and I would integrate it, and hone it to a point, and I would fight these charges completely and totally, and I would not give up until I had won.

Several weeks later, I was arraigned in federal court.

When I walked in, the first thing they did was take me to a small room and fingerprint me like a common criminal. Then they took a mug shot and escorted me back into the huge courtroom.

We sat down and the U.S. Marshall came in and instructed the clerk to read the charges. I was told to stand.

The clerk read out: "The United States of America vs. Timothy Wilkes."

I thought of the Army, the Navy, the Marines, the F.B.I., the entire government. Everything and everyone was against me.

I was charged with three counts: two violations of the Hobbs Act and one count of conspiracy to violate the Hobbs Act. At that point, I began to appreciate Gedney Howe. He was right. I needed him utterly and completely. This was foreign territory, foreign ground and he was the only guide.

By June 1991, I think most of the people in South Carolina were convinced their whole state government was corrupt. A lot of folks thought I was just like the others, that since I was indicted, I had to be a crook, just like everyone else. There was a frenzy building, not only in the federal prosecutor's office, but in the general populace as well. "Let's get rid of all of them. They're all guilty. Let's hang them."

I spent most of my time at home. It had become a silent and lonely place. It had not been like that in the past. Before the federal investigation, my house was busy. Three or four people would stop by, either early in the morning or late at night. Sometimes five or six notes would be stuck in the door. The phone was always ringing, or the answering machine was bubbling with messages. When somebody's son was having trouble getting into college, I would get a phone call asking for help. When there was a big pothole in the center of the street, I would find a note stuck under my windshield wipers. Sometimes, people needed help with electric bills, or food stamps, or entry into a hospital, and they all called me and I loved it.

And all at once, it ceased—all the phone calls, the notes, the people stopping by my house. There was silence. I never thought that silence could be a pain, but it was. I sat in my little house behind the big one and listened to the awful quiet. It was smooth and sharp and cutting. It made me pray. Oh, I had always prayed in my life. My mama taught me that and my Grandma Castles, but the sharp, smooth, hard silence made me pray differently. It made me pray deeply.

All of my life, I thought that prayer was praise, that prayer should be praise and thanksgiving. I had been given so much. I had a quick mind. I had a strong body and a strong will. These were blessings. So when I prayed, it was always to thank God for these talents. I had never asked God for anything. The idea of getting down on my knees and asking God for something seemed blasphemous to me. How in the world could someone who had been given so much kneel down and ask for more? Didn't God give me an intellect? Well, then, I should think my way out of a problem. Didn't God bless me with a stubborn will? Then I should work my way around an obstacle. I thought that asking or pleading was simply wrong. All the tools had been given and all I had to do was use them, and whatever goal I set or problems I encountered, I would achieve or overcome—until now.

I began to realize that I was not in control. All my life I had mistakenly thought that I was in control of my own destiny. Now it was clear that I was not.

For the first time in my life, I felt that I could not handle this problem alone. For the very first time, I felt that all the talents God had given were not enough to extricate myself from this maelstrom.

Deep in the dark of a hot, July night, I went down on my knees. I closed my eyes and prayed: please help me. I don't know what to do. I've never asked you for help before. Was that wrong? Was that pride? I did not mean it as pride. I did not ask you because I thought I should not, but maybe I was wrong. I need your guidance and strength in this matter. Everything could end for me—my whole life. If it is possible, give me the wisdom and the courage to go on and to win. You know my heart. You know I did not do the thing that they accuse me of. Please help me, oh God.

The trial date was set for September 16th and

that black locomotive was almost on me. Gedney and Kenny were working long hours putting together my defense. Kenny came up with two very important ideas. The first was that we should not allow Ron Cobb to stay on the witness stand for hours. Kenny had watched the trials of other legislators and he thought that their attorneys had made a grave error by allowing Cobb to dominate the trial.

"We're going to treat Mister Cobb differently," Kenny said.

"How?" I asked.

"We're not going to give him a lot of time up there."

"Why?"

"Because by just giving him a little time, we are saying to the jurors that he's a nothing, that we're not interested in him, and we'd rather get on with what we have to say."

The second idea that Kenny had was that we needed to focus the jury on my childhood. It was something that I had never thought of. Kenny wanted me to take as much time as I could recounting growing up in Winnsboro as the son of an alcoholic. He wanted me to go through my memories and summon up as many stories as I could about the difficulty of my youth. This later came to be known as the "Little Timmy" defense. I thought that both of these ideas were good. I left my fate in Ken and Gedney's capable hands.

So the days went by. I tried to put on my happy face when I was out in the public. I would go into my office and smile and cut up with my staff and try my best not to let them see my worry and concern. I made myself continue to frequent public functions, even though it was hard for me to do so. I noticed that at every gathering people didn't know how to approach me. They would usually not even speak, unless I did. The first place I sensed this new coldness, this sense of shunning, was the Winn-Dixie in Winnsboro.

Since I am a single person, I never buy a lot of groceries. I go to the store three or four times a week. It is a social place, a grocery store. Some of my best conversations with people have occurred in the Winn-Dixie. I would run into a nurse who's concerned about the safety of the local nuclear reactor, or a teacher who thinks that our schools need more money, or a banker who tells me that campaign reform for all political candidates needs to be implemented promptly. Oh, sometimes I would get a little put out because a ten-minute trip to the store would turn into an hour's stay, but it was fine because I got to find out what people were thinking about.

Anyway, a few weeks after the indictment and all the publicity about it, I noticed that when I entered the Winn-Dixie, people immediately turned away from me. I saw them catch a glimpse of me and then turn their buggies in the other direction. This was another blow. Sure, no one came by the house or called me, and that was hard, but actually seeing people turn the other way as if I had some kind of disease—this was the most difficult thing of all. I hated it. I had spent my whole life trying to help people, and prided myself on shaking a hundred hands a day, and now there were few hands to shake, few smiles to exchange.

I was a pariah.

# 11

Finally, it was September. The trial was only a few days away. Gedney was laying out the strategy of the defense; Kenny was interviewing prospective character witnesses. We used my offices in Columbia for our headquarters. Boxes and boxes of files were everywhere. Everyone got there around 8:30 in the morning. There was coffee and talk. Gedney was really running the show now. At last, I had let him. He barked orders to my secretaries and told everyone what to do and when to do it. We ate lunch in my small conference room. I wanted to go out, but Gedney said it was a waste of time and that we couldn't afford socializing at this point. Every day we ate the same lunch: chicken fajitas and salad. Gedney always ordered. At this point, he even had control of my diet.

We worked on, ten to twelve hours a day. I found myself getting along with Gedney, allowing myself to trust him more and more.

At last, the first day of the trial arrived. So far the U.S. Attorney was 26 and 0. They had not lost a case.

I was incredibly nervous, my stomach full of lumps and bumps, gurgles and hisses. When I walked into my office, Gedney was standing there, his dark eyes sharp and hard.

"What the hell are you wearing?"

"It's a gray suit," I said.

"It's an Italian suit. You look like John Gotti."

"Gedney, this is a very conservative suit."

"I swear to God, Wilkes, you just will not listen to what I say, will you? You need you a plain, brown suit. And where the hell are your glasses? You got to wear them. Jurors like people who wear glasses. It means they're simple, down-to-earth, God-fearing."

"My glasses are broken."

"Where?"

"What? Oh, right at the hinge."

"Good, we'll fix them with a little tape. They'll look even better." Gedney clapped his hands for a secretary. She appeared, and he dispatched her to my house in Winnsboro to get a conservative suit and my glasses.

It was September 16, 1991. The sun was fierce. Columbia was cooking like a pot of grease. Gedney insisted on walking to the federal courthouse. It was only a few blocks from my office. Two blocks into our walk, the sweat was pouring out of us. The sky was clear and I could see a hawk hunting over Main Street. A few wax myrtles were still blooming. I could smell hamburgers frying someplace, and the city sound of traffic and sirens was busy in the air.

I was numb, really. It was like a dream. How could this be happening? How could an innocent man be indicted? How could he actually have to go to trial? Somehow everything had been turned around in

America. I knew that the cornerstone of American justice was a lie. You were not presumed innocent. You were presumed guilty. I watched the brown hawk circling over the street.

We went up the back steps of the courthouse. Just as we reached the top, several reporters saw us. I heard one of them shout, and when he did, a roiling mass appeared and started racing towards us. They were carrying cameras and audio equipment. The door was locked and they caught up with us. There must have been twenty reporters. They shoved the black cameras and the microphones into my face and got as close as they could, so close that I could smell them. They wanted to get their pictures: the beginning of the end of Tim Wilkes.

The door was opened and we disappeared into the coolness of the law.

The courtroom was big and full of echoes. The judge's bench sat at the back. To the left of it were the seats for the jury, and next to them, the table for the prosecution. The prosecutors were there: John Barton, Sherry Lydon, and Clarence Davis. The table for the defense sat on the other side of the room. It was far away, almost in a shadow.

We sat down and I closed my eyes and prepared.

The day was taken up with jury selection. There were over a hundred potential jurors. Each had filled out a questionnaire, which had already been read by the prosecution and the defense. If either side did not like a juror, it could strike him, not allow him/her to sit. We were allowed ten strikes, the prosecution five. The first juror came forward. Gedney's questions were sharp and clear. He wanted to make sure the juror would not convict me.

"Mister Smith, I see, here, you were a detective," Gedney said.

"Yes, sir."

"You believe in the law?"

"Yes, sir."

"You believe that the law is always fair?"

"Most of the time."

"Mr. Smith, over there is sitting my client, Timmy Wilkes. Have you heard of him?"

A smile. "Yes, sir."

"Why you smiling, Mister Smith?"

"I heard Mister Wilkes is in a peck of trouble."

"Strike the juror, your Honor," Gedney said.

Another potential juror came forward and sat down. A young woman.

"Have you ever heard of Operation Lost Trust?" Gedney asked.

"Yes, sir."

"Have you met Tim Wilkes, the defendant?"

"No. Seen him in the paper and on TV."

"Do you think he's guilty?"

"I don't know until I see the evidence."

"Do you believe a person innocent until proven guilty?"

"Yes, sir, I do."

"Seat the juror."

That evening, we all went back to my office. Gedney said he was pleased with the way things had gone. So was Kenny. Gedney had brought in his partner, Alvin Hammer, to help research the case. Hammer would never say a word during the trial. He was there for one primary reason: to lay the groundwork for an appeal if we happened to lose. His presence for this reason bothered me. I knew that "the Hammer" was brilliant, but I didn't like the idea that during the entire trial we were preparing to be defeated.

After we'd talked awhile, Kenny went out to his motor home, which he had driven from Winnsboro and parked outside my office. Gedney and Alvin disappeared into the night.

The next morning, we finished the jury selection.

In the afternoon, the prosecution and the defense made their opening arguments.

The prosecution went after me. Sherry Lydon led the attack. She said I was a liar and a crook, that I was a corrupt politician. She said that I had sold my vote for $1,500 in cash and that I was bribed to pass the pari-mutuel betting bill. She said that the jury would see videotapes of my accepting this cash in exchange for my voting for the bill. She said that because Ron Cobb paid me money, I worked hard to pass the bill.

She said a lot of other things, most of them making me look like a complete scoundrel. Then Gedney got up. His opening statement was brilliant. He looked at the jury, and said that our case was different from all the others they may have heard about. He said that Timmy Wilkes had taken a cash campaign contribution and that it was a legal thing to do. He said that I did not sell my vote, that I spent the money on my campaign and that the defense would prove it. In the course of these remarks, Gedney mentioned several witnesses who would appear on my behalf, among them Ben Gregg and Frank Knapp. Gedney said that before I received the campaign contribution in cash from Cobb, that I contacted Ben and Frank. They were my political and ethical advisors. I had asked them if I could accept the contribution, and they had said it was perfectly legal as long as I reported it and used it in my campaign.

I noticed that Mike Clemens did not like this part of Gedney's statement at all. Clemens was head of the F.B.I. team that set up the sting. Behind him perched a number of F.B.I. agents that he could send out at his will. They were his private flock of investigators to use in any way he saw fit. As soon as Gedney revealed what he did about Ben and Frank, Clemens immediately turned to two of his men and sent them winging out of the courtroom. Later, I found out that these agents went straight to Ben Gregg. I wasn't there, of course, but Ben told me what they said to him, and I envision it as something like this:

"Mister Gregg, I'm John Doe with the F.B.I." He flashes a badge. "I understand you're going to testify for Tim Wilkes?"

"Yes, sir, I am."

"Do you know what perjury is, Mister Gregg?"

"Certainly."

"If you get on the stand and tell a lie to help out your friend in a federal trial, there can be terrible consequences for you."

"I'm not going to tell a lie."

"Terrible consequences, Mister Gregg. The kind of thing you may not ever recover from."

"I'm just going to tell the truth. I'm just going to say what happened."

The agents badgered Ben Gregg pretty good that day, but he stood his ground. There were many other occasions during the trial when Clemens rose up and flung his agents into action. Several times when Gedney revealed a name of someone who was going to help me, the agents roused and hunted. To me it seemed unfair. I didn't have a group of men at my disposal whom I could send out to challenge the prosecution. And why was the F.B.I. allowed to do this in the middle of the trial? Imagine, if you were on the stand, if somehow or another you were accused of a crime that you did not commit. There sits the F.B.I.—the Federal Bureau of Investigation, J. Edgar Hoover's boys, the brightest and the best, and as soon as you mention a friend of yours, bam—the F.B.I. rushes out and tracks your friend down and intimidates the hell out of him. It's not fair. It's not American. Only after the trial did I find out what they had done to a friend of mine whom I will call Spots.

At some point, the F.B.I. had gone to Spots and said that they believed he had some illegal doings with Ron Cobb in 1988. They said Spots had delivered a package to Cobb and that the package contained an illegal substance. Spots was horrified and denied that he had done this, but the F.B.I. pushed him hard. They said they had witnesses and that they would testify against him for distributing drugs, unless—unless—he would tell them everything he knew about Tim Wilkes.

Spots had to hire a lawyer.

The day came for the inquisition. The F.B.I. took Spots into a small room and wired him up to a lie detector. For two and a half hours, they asked him questions about me: Had he ever seen me take illegal drugs? Did he know if I had committed adultery? Had I ever beaten anyone up?

The questions went on and on. My friend said that he had never seen me do anything illegal—except maybe to drive over the speed limit.

When the agents finally took the electrodes off him and he was leaving, they said to him: "Sorry, but you flunked the lie detector."

Spots was stunned. He said that he couldn't have, that he had told the truth. He told the F.B.I. that they would just have to indict him, that he had said all he knew.

As Spots and his attorney began to shuffle from the room, the F.B.I. agent said: "Okay, listen, we were just kidding. You didn't flunk the test. We just wanted to see if you had something else to add. You passed the test."

As I said, it was after the trial that my friend told me this story, but I was still outraged. It revealed to me the lengths the F.B.I. would go to get you, if they wanted you.

Gedney continued with his opening statement. He told the jury that I was going to get up on the stand. That I was an honest and an innocent man and had nothing to fear. He told them that they would hear from Dwight Drake, a lawyer and a successful lobbyist, who well understood the workings of the State House.

He said that the jury would hear from Duby Thompson, who was the legitimate lobbyist for the pari-mutuel bill. He even told them that they would see a videotape of Ron Cobb handing money over to me, and they would see me fold it and stick it into my pocket, and that he would prove that my action was not in any way illegal.

He summed up his opening statement eloquently. Then the prosecution started calling their witnesses—the people that they wanted to prove that I had taken a bribe in exchange for my vote. They were a previously rehearsed prosecution team who had participated in every trial before mine.

The first one up on the stand was Sandy McKinney, who was the Clerk of the South Carolina House of Representatives. They asked her a lot of procedural questions. The prosecution wanted to familiarize the jury with the workings of the House. They asked her to define terms like "running the calendar," "adjourning debate," "roll call vote," etc. There were other expressions that came up in her testimony that the prosecution asked her to explain. Things like: "working your rows" and "getting down in the trenches." They wanted the jury to think that these words were sinister, and that any House member who said, "Yeah, I'm gonna get down in the trenches and work my people" had probably taken a bribe from Ron Cobb, and that these words were an indication of it. Sandy was questioned around 20 minutes, then Gedney began to cross-examine her.

Gedney Howe has a presence in the courtroom. His movements are slow and graceful and deliberate.

He is almost like a dancer. Every motion of his hands, every expression of his face, and posture of his body is done deliberately and intended to have some kind of effect upon the courtroom, no matter how subtle.

With his dark hair beginning to gray and his trim body immaculately straight, he approached the witness gently, softly, so as not to cause alarm, as if to say to her: take it easy, relax, I'm your friend, and you and I are going to have a little waltz together.

"Sandy, have you known Timmy here a good while?"

"Yes, sir. I've known him a long time."

"Does he work hard at what he does?"

"Very hard."

"What's Tim's attendance record in the House?"

"He's never missed a day."

"Now, as Clerk of the House, you sit way up there near the speaker, right? You're high above the chamber?"

"Yes, sir."

"You can see the whole House from where you are?"

"Sure can."

"Do you know where Timmy sits?"

"Yes, sir."

Gedney pulled out a chart and pointed to my desk. "So Timmy sits here. He goes from here to the podium, where he talks to his colleagues. Does he do that often? Does he go to the podium often?"

"He does."

"Does he make speeches, and participate, and

run his mouth a lot?"

"One of the most vocal people in the House," Sandy said.

"So Tim is talkative, and loud, and participatory, and hardworking?"

"Yes."

"Does he work his rows?"

"Yes, sir."

"Does he work his delegation?"

"Yes."

"Does he get people to vote his way on bills if he really believes in them?"

"Yes, sir."

"Anything unusual about that?"

"No, it's what a good House member does."

"So Timmy works his rows, gets down in the trenches, works his delegation, and he does it well?"

"He's one of the best."

"And what he's doing is good?"

"Yes, sir."

"How long have you known him?"

"Ten years or more."

"Have you ever known him to do anything dishonest?"

"No, sir."

"Nothing?"

"Nothing."

Here I began to see the utter brilliance of Gedney's mind. He had taken one of the prosecution's witnesses, one of the people whom they were counting on to build their case, and he had turned her. By subtle and sinuous questions, he had made Sandy McKinney into our witness. Her expertise, her knowledge, her obvious honesty and goodwill and integrity, Gedney had oh, so gently, stolen and laid like a gift, like a boon on our side of the table.

It was an iridescent performance, but it was only the beginning of Gedney's magic.

# 12

After Sandy, the prosecution put up Pam Bennett. I had gone through 12 years of school with her—grammar school through high school. Pam had worked for some time for the South Carolina Tourism Council. The prosecution wanted her to testify so that she could prove that the pari-mutuel betting bill would affect tourism. Obviously, if the bill had been passed, more tourists would come into the state and thus, interstate commerce would be affected, a necessary result if the Hobbs Act was to be invoked.

Pam was asked a number of questions by the prosecution, and then Gedney got a crack at her.

"Miss Bennett, have you known Tim Wilkes a long time?"

"Yes, sir, I have. All of my life."

"Have you ever worked with him as a legislator?"

"I did."

"What bill did you work with him on?"

"The Beachfront Management Bill."

"Did he work hard?"

"He probably worked harder than anyone else. He studied the problems. He came to know it. I think he understood that bill better than anybody in the General Assembly."

"Did he convince other people to support his point of view?"

"He convinced a lot of people."

"Did anybody pay him any money to convince other people?"

"No, sir."

"So Timmy worked as hard as he could, and he convinced other people to follow his point of view, and no one paid him any money to do it?"

"Yes, sir."

Pam Bennett was the last witness of the second day. We went back to my office. I was exhausted. As soon as I got Gedney alone, I began to pour out my feelings to him: my fears, my expectations, my misery. He listened to me a while, then he let me have it.

"I ain't gonna hold your hand, Wilkes. All this stuff you're saying—all this personal stuff—you go tell it to your girlfriend, or Kenny Goode. I don't want to hear it."

"What do you mean?"

"I mean, I ain't your friend. I'm your lawyer. I run your case. That's my job. My job ain't holding your hand and taking your pulse and listening to your misery."

"Oh, thanks a hell of a lot."

"You will thank me one day."

"Oh, will I?"

"Yeah, you will. Now, go grab Kenny and bleed all over him, I got work to do."

It made me furious. How could Gedney be so

cold? Didn't he have even a shred of empathy? Couldn't he see how this was eating me up, how this could be the end of my whole life?

Katherine and I went out to dinner. All I could talk about was the case. I told her that I thought we were doing pretty well, so far. I thought we were scoring some good points and, so far, nobody had laid a glove on us—but that was before I got back to her apartment in Columbia, which had become my haven during the trial.

There I picked up the newspaper. Margaret O'Shea had written a story for *The State*. I couldn't believe what she said. According to her, the prosecution had scored some major points and things were not looking good for me at all. This kind of reporting continued from her and Jeff Miller all through the trial. No matter who testified for me or what good licks we got in, *The State's* reporters always went away convinced that I was losing, certain that I was like all the others, adamant that I was rotten with corruption. It was one of the hardest things I had to deal with during the trial—the press. They were always at my throat, always convinced that I and every other politician was corrupt, and persuaded that I would be found guilty like the 26 others who had gone down before me.

After reading the newspapers and listening to the news, I ranted and fumed a while, then got a shower.

I wanted a drink. Maybe more than any time in my life, I wanted to feel a cool swallow of wine light up my throat and glow into my belly. But I didn't. I had given it up two weeks before. It was one of Gedney's demands. I remembered the conversation with him.

"And there's something else you need to do, Wilkes. You need to stop your drinking."

"You mean cut it down."

"No, I mean stop it."

"It relaxes me."

"You don't need to be relaxed. You need to be tense. You need to be on guard and tense and clear-minded and you can't do that if you're guzzling booze every night. Give the damn stuff up, you understand?"

I had not understood, but I gave it up. Still, right now I was on the verge of taking just one good pull when Katherine walked in the room.

"Tim, I think there's somebody next door," she said.

"So?"

"No, I mean, I think, you know, that, somebody's listening next door."

I immediately became quiet. It would make perfect sense for the F.B.I. to put someone with a listening device next door. They had a cadre of men working for them on my case. It would be a smart thing for them to do. I spoke to Katherine in a whisper.

"Why do you think somebody's there?" I asked.

"I noticed that the curtains were open. No one's lived in that apartment for two months, and the curtains have always been closed, but now they're open. I also heard a noise when you were in the shower."

"What kind of—"

There was a bump, a very small one from the

room next to us. The sound of it made my heart race. I crept to the wall and put my ear against it. I listened for a time, but heard nothing.

The next morning, with little sleep, I got to the office at 7:30. Gedney and Kenny were already there. They had, at this point, taken over the entire office: they had my four secretaries typing, filing, taking dictation and organizing. Even my partners, Gedney had put to work sifting through years of records in my professional and personal life.

I walked in the door and Gedney gave me one of his cold, hard, bright stares.

"You need to take out those contacts and put your glasses back on."

Gedney took off his dark suit coat, folded it, and set it down. He stuck his hands in his pockets. I could tell a story was coming.

"Small details win or lose cases, Wilkes. You think I'm too concerned about them, but you're wrong. Look, a jury has all day long to do nothing but study the defendant. That's what a jury does. They like to study. They like to find something that will help them to see the truth. Give you an example. I was representing a man who had had an accident at work that damaged his eyes. Our closing argument was that the man's vision was so bad, it had cost him his livelihood. He was almost legally blind. Well, I lost the suit. When I went back and thought about it, I tried to figure out what I did wrong. I visualized every moment of the trial—and then I saw it. While I was making my closing argument, the man took his car keys out of his pocket and started playing with them. The jury was watching. The jury was studying, and when they saw him playing with those car keys, they said: Well, he ain't blind, he's still driving his car."

Gedney smiled and started barking orders.

We got all our stuff together and trudged up Assembly Street. I was carrying my files in a plastic clothes basket—Gedney's idea. Just as we rounded a corner, the press appeared. They galloped towards us, holding boxes of food and cups of coffee, clanking equipment and rattling and shouting and waving their hands as if they had never seen us before. They got to us just before we entered the building.

One of them, a tall man with a mole under his eye, whistled: "Hey, Tim, real nice threads. Who died?"

I looked at Gedney.

Another one shoved a black camera into my face, while the woman with him stuck a microphone against my lips. "Tim," she asked. "Are you going to roll over like the rest? Will you plead guilty?"

Another one said, "Hey, Wilkes, how does it feel to be the only one left with a gun at your head?"

And another wearing an earring: "Wow, man, what happened to your hair? You used to be cool."

When we entered the courtroom, we ran right into the Reverend Edward Murphy. He was a preacher that had run against me twice for my House seat. He was a tall man, with a barrel of stomach, and a moustache that always contained small particles of food and spittle. He waved his Bible over his head and pointed at me, his black eyes dead and unmoving.

"Who's that?" Gedney asked.

"Murphy," I said. "He's always around. I've

called him a few names that he doesn't appreciate. His only claim to fame is that he's my nemesis."

We took our seats again in the dark corner where guilty people sit. Ken and Gedney were by my side and Hammer in the back of the courtroom flipping pages of text.

Mike Clemens, the man in charge of the F.B.I. investigation, took the stand.

Gedney approached Clemens with elan. Suddenly, he reached over and slapped Clemens on the leg. It was a blistering shot and the sound echoed in the courtroom. Several people gasped in surprise. "Mister Clemens, I have been wanting to talk to you. You've really done this state a favor. You got Cobb off the streets. We all know what a sleaze bag he is. Speaking of sleaze, you've known him quite a while, haven't you?"

"Yeah, been working with him a couple years."

"Cobb's a pretty smart guy, isn't he?"

"He is."

"He's a charming person?"

"Yep."

"Persuasive?"

"He is."

"Manipulative?"

Clemens looked confused. "Well, now, I don't know if I'd say that."

"Oh, not manipulative? Mr. Clemens, didn't you catch Cobb red-handed in a cocaine deal with twenty thousand dollars on him?"

"Yes."

"Did you give him his twenty thousand dollars

back?"

"Yes."

"When he started to work for you, didn't you give him full immunity from federal and state prosecution?"

"Yes, sir."

"Didn't you also pay him $3,000 a month, plus expenses, for him and his girlfriend to live?"

"Yeah."

"Then you raised him to $4,000 a month, right?"

"Yes."

"Why in the world did you raise him to $4,000 a month?"

The muscles in the massive jaws knotted. "Well, uh, he had a lifestyle he had to keep going or he might, uh, blow his cover."

"Well, when did he blow his cover? When did Cobb's role become public?"

"July 18th."

"What year?"

"1990."

"Well, what's today?"

"September 19, 1991."

"And you're still paying him $4,000 a month and his cover was blown over a year ago?"

"Yes, sir."

"Now, Mr. Clemens, didn't Cobb have a contract with y'all not to use drugs while he was working with you?"

"Yes."

"Uh-huh. Now, tell me, how many times did

you catch him using drugs while he was working for y'all?"

"Seven."

"Seven times he broke the contract while he was working with the F.B.I.?"

"Yes."

"And you're still paying him $4,000 a month to support his lifestyle?"

"Yes."

Gedney turned and looked at the jury, knowingly. "How much income tax did you withhold from Mr. Cobb's paycheck?"

"None."

Gedney raised his eyebrows and then his hands and peered at the jury. "None?"

"None."

I think if Clemens had been a turtle he would have pulled inside his shell.

"Now, Mister Clemens, I'd like to ask you again—is Mister Cobb manipulative?"

Clemens' brain struggled to ascend into the giddy realm known as thought, and his jaws opened only wide enough to whisper: "Yes, sir, I reckon so."

The prosecution called their next witness: Robert Brown. He was a former state legislator, and one of the floor leaders for the pari-mutuel betting bill. John Barton started off asking Brown if it was legal to accept cash contributions. Brown responded, yes, but usually in small amounts, usually not more than a hundred dollars. Barton then asked if he sold his vote for the pari-mutuel betting bill—that is, had he agreed to vote for the bill and get others to vote for it in exchange for money. Brown responded, yes, he had. Of course, the whole idea of these questions was to make me look like Robert Brown—a man who had previously pleaded guilty to a violation of the Hobbs Act.

Then, it was Gedney's turn. He got up carefully. His movements were slow and certain, each of them without a trace of nervousness. He straightened his suit, touched his handkerchief, smiled at the jury.

I glanced towards the back of the room. Alvin Hammer was still bent over some huge book across his knees. Behind him, the Reverend Murphy was pacing the floor, muttering over his Bible as he moved.

Gedney opened a folder and read something, then stroked his immaculate moustache. Unknown to Robert Brown, Gedney had gotten hold of his previous year's campaign financial disclosure form.

"Mister Brown," Gedney said. "You say it's unusual to get a large cash contribution?"

"Yes, sir. It's very unusual to get one over a hundred dollars. Doesn't happen really."

Gedney walked towards him, opening the folder. "Well, what's this? Your disclosure form for last year says that you received a cash contribution for five hundred dollars?"

Brown's face flushed. "Oh, uh, I uh, um, forgot about that."

"Well, now, you testified that you had never received a cash contribution of over a hundred dollars until you were bribed by Ron Cobb. Here's one you got last year for five hundred dollars. Who gave it to you?"

"That's a businessman back in my district."

"And you just happened to forget about it?"

"Yes, sir."

"So is it really that unusual to get a cash contribution of several hundred dollars?"

"Well, no, I guess it isn't really."

Once again Gedney scored. He had taken a hostile witness and, through the prism of his intellect, made him ours.

On the next day, the prosecution put up Robert Kohn, a former state legislator from Charleston. He had been nabbed early on by the F.B.I., just like Ron Cobb. He, too, like Cobb, started working for the F.B.I. in order to save his own hide. He was a man I scorned because he sold out his friends.

Kohn sat down in the witness stand. His mannerisms, his posture, were those of arrogance and contempt. I began to see how right Gedney was about personal comportment. You could dislike Kohn just because of his cockiness and the Judas grin which seeped from his mouth. He was the personification of impudence.

Clarence Davis (third member of the prosecution team) was asking questions of Kohn on the stand. Kohn said that, yes, Tim Wilkes was a bright guy, very hardworking, a tough competitor. He said that he always had the impression, however, that Tim Wilkes would take a bribe if it were offered.

"Well, I'd like to ask you, Mister Kohn—what is it exactly that made you think Tim Wilkes might take a bribe?"

"Well, when Hurricane Hugo hit, I saw in the paper and on TV where he'd gone surfing. That made me think he was reckless, a daredevil, a kind of guy that lived on the edge, the kind of a guy that would take a bribe."

I was completely astounded. I turned and looked at Gedney, and he was astounded as well. Even the jury seemed rather surprised.

I could see Gedney's face and eyes light up. He wanted Kohn. He approached him with delicate steps, his voice soft and sibilant. He asked Kohn a lot of the same questions he had asked others: what kind of a legislator I was; did I work my delegation; did I put together a core group; did I work my rows; was I bright and hardworking; did I get down in the trenches? Kohn agreed to all these things. Then Gedney asked: "Now, tell me again, Mister Kohn, why in the world did you think Wilkes would take a bribe? Did you ever see him take a payoff previously or hear of it?"

"No."

"Did you ever see him play cards?"

I knew what Gedney was getting at. At a local hotel and legislative hangout, The Town House, members of the General Assembly would get together with lobbyists and play cards. Some said that lobbyists would deliberately lose as a means of compensating legislators for friendly votes.

"No."

"Did you ever see him gamble in any way?"

"No."

"Did he hang around with people who did?"

"No."

"Well, then, why in the world would you think this hardworking, bright, competent legislator would take a bribe?"

"As I said, because I read in the newspapers that he went surfing in Hurricane Hugo."

Gedney turned around and looked at the jury and rolled his eyes. "Oh, well, that's certainly a reason to think a man would take a bribe. Everybody knows that. Thank you, Mister Kohn."

# 13

On the fourth day of the trial, the prosecution presented their star, the star of the sting, the star of the press, the star of the greatest misery and mayhem and calumny that had been visited upon South Carolina since the Civil War—Ron L. Cobb.

Cobb was flashy: silk suits, diamond pinky rings, foreign cars and bleached blonds. He was the man everyone had been waiting to hear. He was the man the F.B.I. had caught using and soliciting cocaine. To save himself, he had worked for the F.B.I. and set up the sting in which he offered his friends and colleagues money to vote for the pari-mutuel betting bill.

The halls of the courthouse were jammed on this day. All the press was there. They had cameras and microphones and tape recorders and lights. The Reverend Edward Murphy was frantically pacing back and forth, bumping into tripods, and jostling cameras, as he spat out quotations from Leviticus.

We were ready, too. Alvin Hammer sat beside an escarpment of legal books, his pencil scribbling notes. Kenny Goode carefully arranged a series of papers and occasionally adjusted his bow tie. And Gedney—Gedney sat tall and neat, his face solemn, and cold, and terrible in its complete confidence.

Cobb swaggered to the stand with a gimble to his head, a smirk on his mouth, and a wink in his eyes. Well rehearsed, he was to spend most of the day on the stand. The prosecution wanted him to narrate the two videotapes which the F.B.I. had taken of me. There were television monitors placed all over the courtroom so that all could view the tapes.

The prosecution led Cobb through the tapes, almost frame by frame. The courtroom listened to the audio and watched the action on the tape, which was grainy and blurry in black and white. The tape was so badly shot that it looked like something recovered from Auschwitz or Buchenwald. On this tape, Billy Graham would have come off looking like Jim Baker.

The entire day was spent on Cobb narrating the two videotapes. He made every word, every gesture, and inflection of mine look as bad as he could. Most of the time, I talked about my campaign. I was a new legislator, all of this political business to me was bright and unsullied and exciting, so I loved talking about it. Cobb continually tried to set me up, but I wouldn't shut up. I wanted to keep talking about the political experience that was so important and so new to me. There was one occasion when Cobb handed me money. He counted out the bills and said: "Here, Tim. Have fun with it."

"Yeah, I'll have fun with it. I'll use it to kick Edward Murphy's ass. My advisors have told me I need to beat him so bad nobody will challenge me again."

In another part of the tape, I refer to Reverend Edward Murphy in rather disparaging terms. The reason I said these things was because Murphy was always running against me and printing up derisive fliers and poking his nose in my business. At one point in the tape, as I was talking about my campaign, I looked at Ron Cobb and said of Reverend Murphy: "Yeah, he's nothing but a dickhead, outlaw, Baptist preacher."

I worried that the jury would condemn this characterization of a preacher. It was one of the most uncomfortable moments for me in the trial.

In the back of the courtroom, the Reverend Edward Murphy puffed up and smiled as if to say: "Got you now."

The prosecution went on to reveal everything about Cobb: that he was a drug dealer, a hedonist, a womanizer. They revealed every dark and sordid event in his life, almost as if they were boasting of it. They did this in order to take away any advantage we might get from accusing Cobb of these things ourselves.

After the prosecution had finished with Cobb, Gedney got up. He shuffled a few papers. He adjusted his glasses. He stuck his hands in his pockets and smiled at Cobb, who beamed back. With a gentle step, Gedney went forward.

"Whew, that's a pretty sordid tale, Mister Cobb. Is it all true?"

"Yes, sir."

"Well, let's see now. You had a contract with the F.B.I. not to use drugs, didn't you?"

"Yes, sir."

"And you broke that contract, didn't you?"

"Yes, sir."

"You lied to the F.B.I., didn't you?"

"Yes, sir."

"That makes you a liar then, doesn't it, Mister Cobb?"

"Yes."

"That'll be all, your Honor."

And Gedney took his seat.

Well, the whole courtroom was incredulous and murmuring. They had thought that we would keep Cobb on the stand as long as possible and that we would try to eviscerate him. But Kenny and Gedney both understood that we had to communicate to the jury that we had no respect or use for Cobb's testimony—and that we were in control of the trial. Everyone was surprised, and we wanted them to be surprised because we wanted to make sure that we were, at all times, setting the tempo and the substance of the trial. So far, we had done a good job. We were turning hostile witnesses into friendly ones; we were keeping the prosecution baffled by our logic; and we even circumscribed the testimony of Mister Cobb, which had played such a dominant role in the 26 cases which had preceded us.

We were feeling pretty good. It was Friday morning. We were planning to put up our character witnesses—those people who had known me all my life and believed in the basic honesty of my constitution. I knew that after these witnesses were finished, that I would testify on Saturday. I had been preparing myself for taking the stand for months, and now, I had one more day and a night to polish the nuts and bolts of my presentation.

But then something went haywire. The prosecution, which we had pinned up and cowered, suddenly produced a tactic that we had not foreseen. Something which threw all of our plans away and placed me in grave danger.

On that Friday morning, as soon as the prosecution and the defense took their positions, but before the jury was seated, John Barton rose and said to Judge Hawkins:

"Your Honor, the prosecution would like to ask the court if we may be allowed to question Mister Wilkes along certain lines that have so far not been investigated?"

"What lines are these, sir?"

"We would like to question character witnesses and Mister Wilkes about whether he has made use of—that is, whether he has used drugs, been a drug user in his life."

I was dumbfounded. This was one of the first questions that Kenny and Gedney had asked me in the beginning of our own investigation over a year ago—and the answer was no. The problem was that perhaps the F.B.I. had dug up someone from my college years who would testify that I was some kind of crazed campus dope fiend. Or maybe that one of my ex-girlfriends or wives would simply get on the stand and lie to get even with me.

"Are there any other questions of this kind?" asked Judge Hawkins.

"We might also raise questions concerning adultery and violent behavior."

The judge stated that he needed to see the

prosecution in chambers to make this decision.

After they had left the room, the questions among Gedney and Kenny and me were whispered, but furious.

"Have you been lying, Wilkes?" Gedney asked, his face accusatory.

"No."

"Timmy, are you sure there wasn't a trip, or a meeting, or a party when you might have—"

"No, I haven't done anything, maybe in college. That's all."

When the judge came back in, to our dismay, he said that he would allow this new line of questioning. Gedney immediately stated that we needed some time to gather certain materials since the course of the prosecution had taken a new direction. An hour's recess was granted.

As soon as we got back to the office, we began to quickly assess the damage. There was no doubt that we had taken a hit. The prosecution had hurt us. No one had seen this tactic coming.

"Whatever happens," Kenny said, "whatever we do, we can't let them seize the initiative with this. That's exactly what they're trying to do. Things have been going our way. We've been making big points, we have the momentum, so now they've raised this drug question to rattle us."

"Did a good job, too," Gedney said.

"But we can't let them do it," said Kenny. "We know that one of the reasons the Feds won all the other cases was because they got in control of the game. They made everyone play by their rules and their time. Now, we can't let them steal this thing from us."

Gedney took off his glasses, twitched his shoulders, and looked at me hard. "You don't do drugs, right?"

"Goddamnit, Gedney, I've told you no. No, I haven't done any drugs, except in school a long time ago. You're supposed to believe me. You're supposed to be my lawyer."

"I just want to get it definite."

A secretary tapped on the door. "Lunchtime?"

"Fajitas!" yelled Gedney.

"Hamburgers," I said.

"Fajitas," Gedney yelled again.

"I'll tell you what I think I should do," Kenny said. "I think I should go talk to our character witnesses we got waiting upstairs. I'll tell them to chatter about everything in the world, except matters relating to character."

"Why?" I asked.

"Because if we raise the character issue, the prosecution will be able to cross-examine and say, Would you still feel the same way about Tim if you thought he used drugs," Gedney said.

"I haven't used drugs," I yelled.

"You have used them. You used them in college."

"That was 20 years ago."

"So what? They'll hang you with it. Or maybe they've got something else. Maybe they've got someone who's willing to lie and say they saw you snorting cocaine off the State House steps."

"Why would somebody say that?"

"To get even with you. An irate ex-wife or former girlfriend. Who the hell knows? They just want to get you."

"It would be a lie."

"And it would do every bit as much damage as the truth."

We all took a breather. We shut up and paced around the room. Kenny opened a window. I could smell the hot asphalt of the street. The heat crawled in through the window and began winding its way through the room. I could hear a siren screaming up Elmwood Avenue.

Gedney and I sat over lunch. It bothered me that he ate the fajita with such gusto. How could he, after all these weeks? When he finished, he wiped his clipped moustache, pushed up his glasses, twisted and shrugged his neck at the same time. He got me up from the table and led me into the conference room and shut the door.

"There's something else you could do," he said.

"What?"

"You could end this whole thing."

"A bullet through the brain?"

"You could plead guilty. Daniel called me last night and he's making his final offer."

"Are you serious?"

Gedney looked at me and raised his eyebrows.

"You are serious, aren't you?"

"I'm your lawyer. It's my obligation to let you know that this is your last chance to fold your hand. They have told me if you plead guilty, that they will ask Judge Hawkins to be lenient. If not, they will gut you."

I jumped up from the table. "I am not guilty, goddamnit. I am innocent. How many times do I have to say it. How many times do I have to yell it. Innocent. Let me spell it. I-N-N-O-C-E-N-T. Without blame. Having no guilt."

Gedney spoke quietly. "Then you'll have to take the stand as soon as we go back in the courtroom."

"You mean today?"

"I mean in about 20 minutes."

"But I was supposed to go tomorrow. I was supposed to have tonight to finish preparing."

"You got 20 minutes, if you want to do it."

I turned around and looked out the window.

"How will you answer the drug question?" Gedney asked.

I didn't say anything. I was dazed. Everything had seemed to be going so well. Our plan was working. Our basic strategy of controlling the trial had held until today.

"You have three choices," Gedney said. "You can say, yes, I experimented with drugs in college. No, I never touched the stuff. Or take the Fifth Amendment. If you say yes, the jury will probably forgive you and you could still win the case, but the Feds could bring you up on drug charges later. If you say no and the prosecution produces a believable witness, you could serve time for perjury."

"What happens if I take the Fifth? What if I say whether I smoked pot or not 20 years ago just doesn't matter?"

"If you take the Fifth, you will lose the case."

Gedney got up. "I'm going to make a few

phone calls. We need to leave in ten minutes. Think about it."

The heat of September was rolling in the open window. It had killed all the cool in the room. I pushed the window down and stuck my hands in my pockets. I remembered Mama. "Never give up," she said. "If you're right about something, if you know down in the deepest marrow of your bones that you are right, don't ever give up, no matter what."

Gedney threw open the door and yelled. "All right, Wilkes, what's it going to be?"

"I'm taking the stand."

"If they ask you the drug question, what will you say?"

"I don't know."

"You don't know?"

"Nope."

"Well, you better make up your damn mind."

"If they ask me the question, it's my call."

And then I smiled. I smiled the biggest, deepest smile I had smiled in 14 months.

When we walked into the courtroom, the buzz from the spectators was loud and excited. The room was filled with bailiffs and onlookers and inquirers. In one dark corner, the ever-present Reverend Murphy held his black Bible, probably praying for my demise.

The court was called to order. A couple of motions were made, and I went up to testify. I was not worried so much about the first part of my testimony, direct examination, because Gedney was asking the questions.

He started off quietly, carefully. The first

questions dealt with my childhood. What was it like to grow up the child of an alcoholic? What was it like to start working as a child? How hard was it not to have a father when everyone else did? They were easy questions. We were continuing to develop the "Little Timmy" theme.

After two hours or so of this, Gedney produced the transcripts of the tapes, video and audio. He didn't show the videotapes, because they tended to make me look so bad. He went over the transcripts—the words that went with the tapes—and made sure that the jury understood all of my responses to Ron Cobb, and what I meant and what I didn't mean. It took another three hours to go through the tapes, and finally, it was night and we were at the end of my testimony—at least my testimony under Gedney's questioning.

At the very end of it all, I turned and looked at the exhausted jury and I said, as simply and honestly and quietly as I could:

"Ladies and gentlemen, all I have left to say to you is that I did not break the law. I did not sell my vote. I did not take a bribe."

I paused and looked down, and then looked back up at them, and said: "I swear to God."

At this point, court was dismissed for the day, and Gedney and Kenny and Alvin Hammer and I made our way back towards my office. I was nearly doubled over with all my files and records. Gedney always insisted that I carry them. I was wearing my cheap suit. My hair was cropped and looked dull brown, and I wore my broken glasses fastened with a wad of tape, and I was carrying the plastic clothes basket full of the worst misery of my life.

Back in my conference room, Gedney excluded all my partners and staff and slammed the door.

"All right," he said. "We go get a little supper and we meet back here at 9:30 tonight and we get ready for your cross-examination tomorrow. It won't be easy."

"Gedney," I said. "Let's just meet real early in the morning. I'm so tired—"

"We meet tonight at 9:30. And don't drink at dinner."

He got up and left.

I went to Katherine's apartment, consumed with apprehension and desire. It seemed that the more tense and uncertain things became, the more I needed her. We made love hard and fast. At 9:30, my face red and beaming, I returned to my office to meet Gedney. He looked at me in a knowing way, then went through the transcripts of the tapes one more time.

After about two hours, Gedney got up to go make a phone call. I glanced at Kenny Goode. He was about as tired as I had ever seen him. His red bow tie had wilted, his brown bangs were dishevelled across his forehead, even his glasses looked tired—the lenses foggy and smeared, and the frames at an odd angle on his nose.

"You look like hell," I said.

"You don't look so good yourself."

"What do you say we book it and go get a quart of tequila?"

"You get tequila, I'll get a six pack of Yahoos."

"You know something," I said, "you've never

really told me why you don't drink."

"It diminishes my already limited grey matter."

We laughed a little, then were quiet.

"Gedney told me something about you," Kenny said. "He told me a couple weeks ago, but I didn't say anything to you. I think you need to know it. Gedney knows you're innocent. He told me he never says that to a client even if he's sure of it, but he said after he had gone through everything and interviewed all the witnesses, he was certain you were innocent."

It did something to me. It was exactly what I needed to hear at that moment, and I knew as soon as I heard it that Kenny had saved it for me. He had saved it for the time when he felt I needed a boost. This is what makes a great lawyer—knowledge and courtroom skill, and all that, but this humanity, this intuitive faculty that allows a lawyer to look into his client and say: all right now, we need a little compassion, or a little sweetness, or we need to kick ass, or vituperate, or threaten, or we need to light a little candle of hope—this gentle art is what makes a good lawyer a great lawyer and a good friend, and I saw it in Kenny Goode that night.

Gedney returned and he and Kenny and I went over things one more time. When we were through, Gedney looked at me.

"Go home, try to sleep, but I want you to remember one thing tomorrow: if you get in trouble on the stand—and believe me John Barton's going to do everything he can to get you in trouble—don't you look over here at me. It'll make the jury think you've been coaxed, or you're guilty, so don't even turn your eyes in my direction. There's not a damn thing I can do for you. You're on your own."

# 14

When I got home to Winnsboro, I went straight to bed. I tossed and wallowed and fluffed and adjusted and curled and straightened.

Around 3:30 in the morning, I got up and walked outside. It was still hot. The katydids were singing in the pecan trees, and I could smell the sweet scent of tea olive. I walked into the garden, through the bright singing of crickets, passed the granite wall where Mrs. Harmon and I talked on so many occasions, and finally out to Vanderhorst Street. This was the place I played when I was a kid. Down the block was the library where I first read Emerson and Thoreau. I looked towards Main Street, where I swept out the pharmacy, and then to the moonlit bricks of the old town clock. It was my town, my place under the shattered, lovely light of the stars.

I wondered if I would survive tomorrow. I wondered if Barton was going to ask me the question about drugs? What would my answer be? Yeah, I did a little dope in college. Or no, I never touched a thing. And then would he produce some enemy: an ex-wife, an old girlfriend, a foe from the General Assembly, and would he or she accuse me of selling cocaine by the pound, heroin by the ton?

Would tomorrow be the end of me?

Would it?

As soon as we got in the courtroom the next morning, but before the jury was brought in, Gedney stood and asked Judge Hawkins whether or not he was definitely going to allow the prosecution to raise the drug question. The judge addressed the question to Mister Barton, who replied that he reserved the right to ask that and all other questions concerning morality and ethics.

Now, Judge Falcon Hawkins is a handsome and solemn looking man, the picture of what a judge should look like: a little silver hair, clear and fresh skin, a sharp nose, and eyes that fire at the hint of chicanery. At this moment, his eyes were spitting.

"I will allow this line of questioning, Mister Barton, but let me make one thing extremely clear. If you ask such questions, you had better be ready to produce the witness who has made statements providing the foundation for the questions. Because if you don't, two things will happen. One: I will declare a mistrial; and two: I will have you, sir, body and soul."

Maybe those weren't his exact words, but they were pretty close.

With that, the jury was called forward, and I took the stand.

John Barton had the hair, suit and demeanor of an ambitious young bureaucrat. He started out hard and rough. He called me a liar and a thief, and a man who was corrupt to the deepest part of my soul. After he spent a while vilifying me, he then pursued accounting questions—pretty boring stuff, really. Why did I record this? Why didn't I record that? After about an hour, he came to a rather amusing part.

"Now, look, Mister Wilkes. I have a record here of a number of names. A number of people, Mister Wilkes. One of your contentions during this trial is that you paid most of the money Ron Cobb gave you, you paid out most of it in cash. If that is the case, why did you pay these people by check?"

I knew I had him. "Well, now, sir, you see those people, those children were in Miss Willa Sims youth group. They had helped pass out fliers in my election. Willa brought me a list of names to my office so I just wrote them checks. I had also promised them that I would take them to see Nelson Mandela in Atlanta. After my election, I rented a bus and we all went down to hear Mister Mandela, who gave about the most inspiring speech I think I've ever heard."

This did not sit well with Mister Barton at all. I began to notice that his heretofore perfect coif began to fray, a few strands went askew, and the brightness of his eyes dimmed. He turned, went to his desk, and then grabbed something out of his pocket, and came at me almost furiously.

"On April the eighteenth, Mister Wilkes, isn't this what Ron Cobb did to you? Isn't this how he paid you off?"

And with that, Barton began slamming down one hundred dollar bills.

"One hundred, two hundred, three hundred, four hundred, five hundred, six hundred, seven hundred, eight hundred, nine hundred, one thousand dollars. Isn't this the way it was done, Mister Wilkes? Isn't this the way he paid you off?"

"No, sir, you see it wasn't a payoff, it was—"

"And how about on May the fifth, didn't Ron Cobb then give you—"

He started again. "One hundred, two hundred, three hundred, four hundred, five hundred dollars for your supporting the pari-mutuel betting bill?"

"No, sir, he was laying down a campaign contribution. That is the truth. That is what I know to be the truth."

Barton grabbed his money and began a new set of questions, but he was not the same cocky fellow that he had been earlier.

Still, I was worried. I thought that at any moment he was going to ask the drug question, and I was not sure what my answer would be. I was certain that I would not lie, but I did not know how I would approach the truth.

But the hours went on and on, and Barton was asking me the same questions, sometimes three and four times, and it began to become clear to me that he wasn't going to ask the drug question, and the reason he wasn't going to ask it was because it was all a bluff. He didn't have a witness ready to accuse me. He didn't have anything at all and he knew it and I knew it.

Finally, the day was over. It was seven o'clock in the evening. I had been on the stand for almost eight hours, and I had not broken, and there had been no drug questions, and I think all of us—Gedney, and Kenny, and I—I think all of us saw that the prosecution had done their best, and failed.

I followed Gedney out of the courthouse.

"Well, Wilkes, since we dodged the drug

question, all you could get now is six years for violation of the Hobbs Act. Not bad."

I noticed there was a smile on his face and a spring to his step. I was glad to have dodged the drug bullet, but the possibility of six years in jail didn't make me feel exuberant.

Sunday night was easier for me. I slept better, but I was not sure of victory. I was still worried that they might have something else to use against me. The paranoia persisted.

On Monday morning, Gedney put on the stand all my character witnesses. There were people who had known me and loved me and nourished me all my life in Winnsboro—people like Quay McMaster, Taft Henry, Maude Ross, Polly Parker, Freddie Cohens, and many others. We had people testify like Dwight Drake and Duby Thompson, both of whom stated that I had supported the pari-mutuel bill long before I ever heard of Ron Cobb. One of the last character witnesses to testify was Barbara Harmon. She talked for a long time, and told the story of my Mama, and the great sadness of Mama's life. She also talked about the death of her own son, Stewart, who had been like a kid brother to me, and she spoke of his early passing, with grace and tenderness. Mrs. Harmon's testimony had so affected Kenny that he got tears in his eyes because he knew Stewart and Mrs. Harmon. He took a handkerchief out of his pocket and wiped his eyes. The judge called for a short recess.

During the break, Kenny ran into Mike Clemens in the bathroom. Clemens looked at him and said: "I saw you sitting there wiping at your eyes. It made me want to puke. I felt like taking out my gun and blowing your goddamned head off."

Kenny told me this story later. I couldn't believe it. The F.B.I. wanted to get me so badly it made no difference to them if I was innocent. They just wanted another trophy. This point was made clear to me about two months later when I heard that Clemens was walking around the State House in Columbia trying to get hold of the business cards of all the lawmakers that the F.B.I. had convicted. He told people that he wanted to get as many cards as possible so he could make a nice collage, frame it, and hang it on his wall.

# 15

Late Monday afternoon, it was time for closing arguments. As usual, the prosecution went up first. Barton was fired up. He ranted and raved and accused me of everything dark and sinister, corrupt and vile and poisonous.

Then, it was Gedney's turn. This surely was his shining hour. He was eloquent, his voice a Broad Street, Charleston susurration, his body moving with grace and sureness across the stage of the courtroom. He talked about the childhood of Little Timmy, the pain and agony of it. He recapitulated my hardworking years in college, and how I had supported my mother. He relived my mother's death, and my rise in the business world, and my complete obsession with the plight of the poor and the weak and the powerless. Then pausing, his voice falling softly, sinking to something like a whisper, he spoke of Ron Cobb.

"And here was Little Timmy, a new, naive, state legislator still talking about helping out poor people, still working for better education and better health care, here was Timmy living a life of service and integrity, unknowing that at that very moment Mister Cobb was beginning to spin his black web, spitting out of the poisonous tumescence of his belly the golden strands of seduction that would lure so many to such a dark end. It was Cobb the spider, Cobb the seducer, Cobb the pernicious predator who threw a sticky filament towards Timmy Wilkes—a filament which returned empty." I don't know if those were his exact words, but it was masterful oratory, and the jury was held as if by an incantation.

When Gedney had finished, the prosecution had one more rebuttal. The judge carefully instructed the jury, and then it was over. The trial was over. Now I had to await the verdict.

Late in the evening, we went back to my office, one last time, and Gedney told me something that completely astounded me, something that I would have never anticipated.

You see, I was convinced that we had won. I was completely sure that Kenny Goode's and Gedney Howe's perspicacity and logic and strategy, and my own innocence, had worked together to win, to vindicate me.

Gedney sat down. He took off his glasses and wiped the lenses. His black hair seemed more silver since we had started working 14 months earlier.

"There's something I want you to do tonight. I want you to go home and be alone. I don't want Kenny there, or Barbara Harmon, or your girlfriend. I want you to sit alone, and I want you to prepare yourself to lose this case."

I stared at him.

"You've got to remember what we have going against us. 26 people have either pleaded guilty or been convicted. The judge—fair man that he is—is sick of hearing the same stories of greed and corruption. The jury—honest and good people that they are—are sick to death of seeing Ron Cobb counting out thousands of dollars in bribes. We have everything in the world going against us. So, you go home and you tell yourself, I'm gonna lose tomorrow. I'm gonna lose, but I will keep my dignity, and my pride, and I will leave that courtroom with a sense of grace. Do you understand me? Timmy?"

I got up and left. I didn't even look at him. I drove home slowly. No radio, no stereo, no stop for a beer. I drove with both hands on the wheel of my truck, up the hills of Winnsboro. Up to the stands of walnut trees and wisteria and the ancient rows of boxwoods.

I went into my little house and I sat all night, still not believing what Gedney had said. Still not understanding. Lose? Prepare yourself to lose? How was that possible? We had demolished them. We had destroyed their arguments, turned their witnesses, confounded their tactics. How could we lose?

These thoughts, and many others, turned in my mind all night, until I saw the first light peeping through the great, round, body of the tea olive outside my bedroom window.

I remembered the ancient line of scripture: "My spirit was poured out like water."

We were back in the courtroom at ten o'clock on Tuesday, September 24, 1991. The judge instructed the jury and sent them away to deliberate. We asked if we could go to my office, because it was near and more comfortable.

We had not been there 20 minutes when the phone rang. The judge ordered us back. The jury wanted a point clarified.

In the courtroom, we went over a part of the videotape and transcript in which the jury was unsure of my answer. Gedney made them see the sense of my reply, and then we were off to my office, and no sooner there, than the phone rang again.

I felt as if the ringing of it pierced my bones, as if the bells rang through my very being.

Gedney answered, gave a quick yep, nope and yep.

"They want more information."

"Oh, no," I said. "I can't keep doing this. About what? They want more about what?"

"You'll find out," Gedney said, and off we went again.

The courtroom was familiar, but different. I felt something new about it. Something unexpected. I looked at the jurors, and I could see light in their eyes.

The foreman of the jury stood. I realized this was it, all of the agony was about to end—one way or another. My heart stopped beating.

"Have you reached a verdict, sir?" Judge Hawkins asked.

"Yes, sir, we have."

"Please read it."

"We find the defendant Timothy C. Wilkes—innocent of all charges."

The back of the courtroom exploded with applause and whistles and yells.

Judge Hawkins banged his gavel and said that

the demonstrations must stop. He thanked the jury, dismissed them, and then he looked me hard in the eye.

"Young man, I want to congratulate you on your demeanor during this trial. It was an arduous affair, and you acquitted yourself well. I also want to congratulate your attorneys on a well-fought and well-presented case."

The judge then turned his eyes to the prosecution. "As for you gentlemen, I offer my condolences, if condolence is the right word—because everybody wins if justice is done. In this case, I have no doubt that justice was done."

Judge Hawkins looked at the crowd in the courtroom. "Y'all can celebrate now."

And celebrate they did.

At that moment, Gedney reached over and touched my hand. Even in my state of euphoria, I was shocked at this most human, most gentle gesture. He said to me quietly, "I want you to sit still a minute. Just sit still and be quiet. There will never be another moment in your life like this. There will never be another time when it was all or nothing. Savor it."

I did as he said. I sat listening to the yells and applause behind me, looking at the tired, but merry faces of the bailiffs, watching the countenance of the prosecution sour and curdle into blackness, feeling the hand of my old friend, Kenny Goode, slide into my own, his eyes very bright.

And not far away, in a small town, in a paintless old house, I saw someone else, young once more, her body, trim and strong, her hair lovely in twilight, her face holding a smile as fresh as the world.

# Epilogue

As of April 1, 1995 over 50 state legislators in three states had been indicted and convicted as part of the F.B.I.'s nationwide investigation of vote buying.

So far, Tim Wilkes, Democrat, of Fairfield County, South Carolina, is the only person to be acquitted of these charges.

## Other Books by Ben Greer

Slammer

Halloween

Time Loves a Hero

The Loss of Heaven